ORION TOO

BILL WONDERS

authorHOUSE®

AuthorHouse™
1663 Liberty Drive, Suite 200
Bloomington, IN 47403
www.authorhouse.com
Phone: 1-800-839-8640

First published by AuthorHouse   8/21/2008

ISBN: 978-1-4389-0412-2 (sc)
ISBN: 978-1-4389-0413-9 (hc)

Library of Congress Control Number: 2008907790

Printed in the United States of America
Bloomington, Indiana

This book is printed on acid-free paper.

In memory of:

Patricia D. Wonders

A great teacher, exemplarily mother
and remarkable leader by example

Drawings and sketches
employed throughout this book
have been provided by:

Eric W. Wonders
Chardon, Ohio

Beginning Notes and Comments

Writing this book has been a truly enjoyable learning experience from the start. My intention has been to keep it casual and conversational yet convey a message that will help any reader better understand the complex environment of people management. I submit that this is a business/people management book that masquerades as a hunting story. In life we humans are all hunters and my writing approach, while unique, marries well with how we live at home and on our jobs. On this adventurous and sometimes dangerous journey I reflected back on important people management issues both serious and humorous. While basically a book for business leaders, it will appeal to readers with interests in travel, hunting and outside adventure. This book's unique approach to people management concepts will please human resource professionals at all levels of any organization. It will hold a special appeal to those thousands impacted by business downsizing, job loss and/or early retirement.

I have been cautioned that an appeal to such a broad audience might distract some readers, and should consider changing the focus to perhaps only professionals engaged in the people management business. Though a wise suggestion, people management is what all of us do every day of our lives: at home, at a department store, at school, at work or out and about. People management skills are important to every human on the planet, and I reserved the right to send my message, written in a way that will interest people from all walks of life.

While reading this if you encounter technical human resource (HR) jargon that is a little confusing or difficult to understand, please read on as the book's message can be appreciated with or without a technical background in HR (Remember too that what we do in HR can be confusing to everyone).

Throughout my writing I provide quotes and references that support or qualify the written words of the text. In each case I am careful to identify the source and author and only one instance was I obligated to resort to the author as "unknown." The information used has been collected by me from books, newspapers, magazines, management association bulletins, business flyers, or technical publications throughout my HR career. Credits are provided as accurately as possible.

It is important for the reader know that every story I tell in this book is true. I speak with frankness and honesty about the good and the bad. Writing in this way, an author must recognize that telling the truth about people and/or organizations is often a painful revelation and hard to accept. Since I am not writing to embarrass anyone or any organization, I have elected to use some pseudonyms throughout my text. In each instance I have provided my qualification to the name or organization used.

Constellation Orion

The Hunter in the sky

In Greek Mythology Orion, son of Poseidon, God of the Sea, was a mighty hunter who had cleared the kingdom of wild beasts. The mythological stories regarding Orion carry some conflicting claims; however each story recognizes that Orion was a great hunter, and upon his death a constellation was named in his honor.

The Orion Constellation is an oblong configuration with three bright stars in line near the center. These bright stars are easily identified and visible to the naked eye on a clear night and represent Orion's belt. The brightest and largest of Orion's stars is Betelgeuse, with its position in the sky identified as the hunter's right shoulder.

In the Northern Hemisphere, the Orion Constellation is visible from late fall through early spring and is one of the constellations that even this author can identify with relative ease.

CONTENTS

CHAPTERS IN ADDENDUM
Principles of sound HR Management

CHAPTER 1

TIME TO CHANGE
(BUSINESS IN THE GLOBAL ARENA)

"Life is a mystery to be lived,
not a problem to be solved"

Dr. Dave Smith, Ph D.

The new millennium arrived, and we were subjected to the age of massive industrial machinations. Downsizings, layoffs, restructurings, mergers, and company closures were the order of the day as we confronted changes in the new global marketplace. I am convinced that people worldwide have been affected in some way (positive or negative) or have a relative or friend who has gone through change generated by this massive wave of industrial plethora. A day rarely passes that we don't read in the paper about more jobs lost and careers eliminated due to these changes. In a recent newspaper article a major retail pharmacy corporation announced that they had reached agreement to purchase a company engaged in mail order prescription drugs. In that corporate merger the two companies declared that they will save four hundred million dollars in "operating synergies." Synergy is the new word that we corporate folks use to euphemistically describe, among other things, job eliminations. With synergy we do not need two accounting departments, we do not need two finance departments we do not need two sales departments, two HR departments, two purchasing departments, and so on. When we synergize in the corporate world these days the synergizing process means that thousands of jobs and careers come to a screeching halt.

Admittedly, in my career I was personally called on to assemble a number of synergy projects, and most of those workforce reduction scenarios occurred in the last three years of my employment. Then, at age sixty-one, I reached a point where it was appropriate to synergize myself!

Most recently, I was employed as Vice President of Human Resources for a global Ohio-based manufacturing company. This company had been my employer for twenty five years and had been in the manufacturing business for 104 years (past tense). To briefly summarize my work with this organization I can say, without qualification, that it was an excellent company to work for, those twenty-five years were truly enjoyable and the time passed by ever so fast. My work involved extremely interesting domestic and overseas assignments with countless rewarding and fun experiences. Over the years, I had direct involvement and management responsibility in employment, staffing, college relations, labor relations, training, salary administration, benefit plan design, and was also given responsibility to manage a small manufacturing division. Most of all, my career was a tremendous, ongoing learning experience.

Unfortunately, our manufacturing company confronted the same major competitive problem that numerous other U.S. manufacturing companies faced regarding the unbalanced trade with China. The sad truth is that in this new millennium, all U.S. manufacturing organizations will sooner or later be up against the $1.03 per hour average wage and twenty-eight cent benefit cost for labor in China (per 2004 industrial survey). It caught up to my company, and too much of my own work evolved into unending reorganizations, plant closures, layoffs, and finally, a total company shutdown. It was my unwanted responsibility to be the person delivering bad employment news to thousands of very good people. Then, of course, once all terminations were completed and no "humans" remained, I could not argue that the company no longer had a need for a Human Resources Vice President. As Curly Howard of the "Three Stooges" was fond of saying: "I'm a victim of circumstance."

> *"The trouble with the rat race is that*
> *Even if you win, you're still a rat."*
>
> *Lilly Tomlin*

I honestly viewed this new freedom from the synergizing rat race as a refreshing change and unique opportunity. There were no phones ringing, no meetings, no crises to manage (that were at times unending), no corporate travel, no more layoffs or shutdowns, and no more work-related stress. This new circumstance laid the groundwork to launch into new and exciting adventures, to change career direction, take time to relax, and also time to identify and conquer new goals.

Throughout my life I was always a goal-oriented person. My goals were long-term, short-term, and even conspired daily with ever present "To-Do" lists at work and "Honey-Do" lists at home. Whatever the circumstance, I selected my goal (disregarding the nay-sayers), prepared my plan to achieve it, and then stuck to it through completion. As I looked at organizing some goals for my next journey in life, I wanted to first undertake an activity that would clearly define and symbolize the end of one long journey and the beginning of an entirely new adventure. It needed to be an experience that would vividly delineate this change in direction.

REFLECTIONS

"If you think you can or
If you think you can't,
You're always right."

Henry Ford

Reflecting back, I thought about a number of things that I previously wanted to try but for some reason (some circumstance) did not set out a goal or plan for achievement. What I decided to do was to organize all those ideas by setting up my own single-person brainstorming session to surface all potential experiences and then attempt to prioritize the entire mess.

Most of my unrealized experiences involved travel. A trip to mainland China was something I thought would be grand. Travel first to visit the port city of Shaing-hai to experience the economic and human chaos of that major world metropolitan area, then on to Beijing to experience the order and beauty of China's capital city, followed by a visit to the relatively unblemished interior with stops at places near Nan King. Hey, I might even take time out to see where so many U.S. jobs had went.

Another possible sojourn was to travel through Mongolia. It may sound crazy to consider a journey through Mongolia, as it is not your typical travel destination, and I doubt that the country has ever produced a travel brochure and may not have a single vacation resort within its boundaries. However, based on everything that I read and knew about Mongolia it seemed to be a nation of nothing - a nowhere place on earth that was unquestionably foreign to everything I have ever experienced and would certainly bring a sense of appreciation for the lifestyle we take for granted at home.

There had always been the draw of Australia as well … the great land down under. Australia, a nation of incredible character, would be a fascinating place to see and experience. My plan, if I journeyed to Australia, would include seeing some of the outback country, the Great Barrier Reef, and the cities resting within the mountains of the great dividing range as well as visits to the many ocean sites along that continents beautiful eastern shore. Some ocean fishing would be an added plus for such a journey.

As an ex-soldier and military history buff, I also thought it would be rewarding to arrange my own travel through Western Europe primarily to visit some of the military battlefields of historical wars. The continent of Europe is not new to war and to name a few: there was the Seven Years' War, the Thirty Years' War, the 100 Years' War, the Napoleonic Wars, the Crimean War, the Great Northern War, the War of the Grand Alliance, the many Civil Wars, Wars of Succession, the Crusades as well as the carnage of World War I and World War II. European conflict continues to this day in places like the Balkans. There are factions in Spain philosophically prepared to regenerate that country's last civil war that (supposedly) ended in the late 1930s. Yes, Europe would be a phenomenal place to visit for anyone interested in learning more about war and conquest.

Once this brainstorming was completed and ideas prioritized I had to decide what among those unrealized experiences would be the best one to be undertaken now and most importantly to get it done before it simply was too late. The potential new-experience list was a long one as dozens of ideas and remembrances came to mind. My selection was made more complex as my priorities seemed to be in a constant state of flux. Life occurrences such as job loss and/or retirement harbor the ability to throw your mind into a temporary state of disorder and chaos!

Throughout my brainstorming however there was one learning experience I dreamed of throughout my early school years that continued to creep back into my thoughts surfacing ahead of all others, and this one fitted the need. It was a dream to further explore the last wilderness frontier in Alaska.

Early explorers had always fascinated me. Courageous adventurers setting off into new worlds and visionaries who would look beyond the horizon then set off to explore the mysterious unknown were the people I read about and revered in my youth. I admired those bold new world adventurers like Christopher Columbus, the fearless Vikings and idolized, self-reliant new-frontier scouts like Admiral Byrd and Roald Amunsen.

Pioneer path finders like Daniel Boone and the incredibly adventurous team lead by Lewis and Clark were the role models I always held in special fascination. The people I admired most as a youth were those visionaries who could hunt, live off the land, and were always looking beyond the present, discovering new lands and exploring new frontiers. Most of all they were individuals courageous enough to launch exploration drives even when conventional thinking advised them not to venture forward. They had vision and they were brave.

For earthbound folks our planet, absent the deep sea, harbors few new worlds open for individual exploration. Few new frontiers remain that had not been at least partially explored. Only areas of Alaska retain the image of a last frontier, awaiting further exploration.

"It gets late early out there"

Yogi Berra

EARLY DAYS

My father was an outdoor person who took me hunting and fishing from the time I began to walk. He not only taught me hunting and fishing skills but outdoor survival skills as well. I learned how to track animals, set traps, find food growing in the forests, how to build a shelter for cover, make a fire without matches, keep warm in the cold, and find my way through unfamiliar outdoor surroundings. Consequently, his teachings helped me become a man who has always been very comfortable in the outdoors and at home in the woods. It was my good fortune, over the years, to have had so many memorable fishing and hunting experiences with my late father.

The one unrealized learning experience that floated through my head as a young man and the one that now stood out above the others was a challenge or dream I had to drive the famous Alcan Highway to Fairbanks, Alaska, get as far back into the "Last Frontier" as possible, and hunt a moose. Not just a moose - the largest member of the deer family and the largest game animal in North America - but an Alaskan Moose from the central part of Alaska, an area that grows the biggest moose in the world. It was this unrealized experience that I finally determined would be a perfect start for this new journey in life.

If no one else, certainly Orion, the mythological greatest hunter, would look at this decision with great favor although I recognized that few earthbound humans thought my transitional travel plans were all that clever.

Aerodynamics and physics employed by Alaskan bush airplanes had always fascinated me, and even at an early age I recognized that going anywhere into the true, rarely explored areas of the Alaskan Frontier, was best done using a small bush airplane for transportation. Exploring the last frontier by road would be very limited as there were few roads available for use, hiking also presented limitations in range of operation, as Alaska is so great an expanse, any boat exploration, while better, still limited travelers to useable waterways. An airplane modified to operate off short, rough landscape, lakes, or rivers (a bush plane) opened up all the horizons in the last frontier and could get you into essentially anywhere: mountains, lakes, rivers, boreal forests, or tundra.

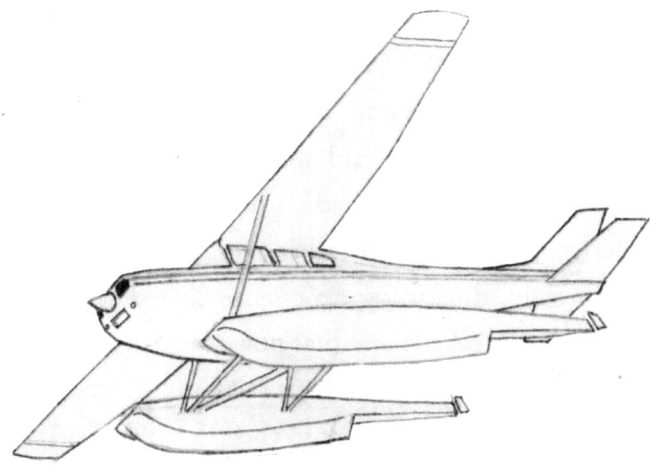

Bush planes including float planes are invaluable in Alaska

Over the years I learned to fly airplanes, earned a private pilot's license, and had the good fortune to visit Alaska on several occasions going back to 1973. Nevertheless, I had never driven the famous Alcan Highway to get there, and I had never hunted an Alaskan Moose. With my time no longer restricted by the pressure cooker of business management, I could begin my new journey, severing the past and beginning the new, by leisurely fulfilling that early travel and hunting dream.

With my decision made, to the initial dismay of my wife of thirty-four years, a new journey would begin with new goals and an action plan for another great learning experience in this fantastic mystery called life. On this journey I could also take my time and enjoy every minute of the travel and even take time out to stop and smell the flowers along the way as there were no critical time schedules, no planes to catch, no meetings to attend, and no more business management issues to address.

The long travel time on this first new journey would also provide me with an opportunity to reflect back on my career in Personnel/ Human Resource Management. Time would be available to comment on some of the dramatic changes that I had witnessed taking place in the workforce and society, plus share my thoughts and a few experiences regarding the business of people management.

Alaska Moose – largest game animal in North America

CHAPTER 2

PREPARATION FOR DEPARTURE
(PLANNING AND LOGISTICS)

"Anyone who stops learning is old, whether at 20 or 80.
Anyone who keeps learning stays young.
The greatest thing in life is to keep your mind young."

Henry Ford

At Elm Road Elementary School my Cub Scout Pack 222 motto was to "Be Prepared." I believed it then, and to this day, I am an advocate of ample preparation prior to the execution of any important activity. Planning and preparation would be the foundation for success on this new journey no different than a solid foundation being the basic component needed for the construction of any quality building.

A few years after completing my bachelor degree I found myself working as the Plant Personnel Manager for a very large New York City based world-wide manufacturing company. This company was an organization absolutely driven by numbers. The company chairman was, in my opinion, a business genius and certainly a legend in his own time, pioneering the building of a mega U.S. corporation in the late 1960's and early 1970's. This was where I learned to prepare and execute business plans, long-term plans, annual plans, quarterly plans, and plans for each and every workday. I learned that business plan preparation was important even if you thought through an activity, wrote out your plan, then placed it in your desk never to see it again.

In business it was always imperative to think through the work that lies ahead, plan your course of action and consistently execute the plans you design.

One poor planning/preparation experience I witnessed at this company took place at one of our semi-annual business meetings where an executive and direct report to the chairman was in attendance. Our plant controller, who was a great guy, had to present some numbers on behalf of our general manager and these numbers were just a little "hokey." Not dishonest, but not 100 percent correct in their business interpretation/application, and a clever presentation was needed to mask over our business unit's recent sub-par performance.

Unfortunately, our controller didn't go to the meeting fully prepared. He was a bright individual and did put together several overhead slides for this meeting but no special planning or preparation regarding these questionable figures. With confidence he said to other staff members prior to the meeting that he didn't really need anything special and he would "wing it" with the data. His meeting presentation went very well until the end when he started to gather up his notes to return to his seat. The executive visiting from NY Headquarters, who was silent throughout the presentation, stopped him and asked that he put up one of his prior overhead slides (I seriously think the NY guy had memorized all of them). He had questions on that slide that lead to more questions on other slides he asked to see, and before he was over with his questioning, this part of the meeting took the form of a one-on-one inquisition leaving our controller physically and professionally destroyed.

It was brutal, and this happened right before the eyes of everyone on our staff. Only one person in the meeting could have spoken on behalf or in support of the controller, and that was our Division General Manager who, I am sure for reasons of self-preservation, elected to remain silent. It was a case of a lamb being lead to slaughter in corporate America and a valuable lesson for me regarding preparation. Scout Pack 222 was right!

PREPARATION OF HUNTING GEAR

Here was an area where you genuinely cannot simply wing it, and I quickly learned that my big-game hunting gear had fallen into a sad state of affairs. Clothing for this type of hunt must protect the hunter from the weather (rain, snow, wind and sun) and must support the hunter's requirement for concealment (camouflage), scent masking, and noise abatement. As an example, a plastic poncho would do a great job of keeping the rain off a hunter, but the smooth material surface is visible (even the type with a camouflage print), it could be difficult to wear while hunting, and most of all, it would be very noisy. Every move a hunter makes wearing this stiff plastic cover generates a noise that is clearly telegraphed throughout the woods to sound-sensitive wild game (like deer). A plastic poncho works to keep the rain at bay and is cheap, as the cost is only a few dollars compared to several hundred dollars for the recommended hunting attire, but it would give away your presence in the woods with every move made. The expensive hunting attire is warm, will keep you dry and yet is made of a soft material that makes little or no noise. Nearly all of my hunting and camping gear needed to be replaced before I started this hunt. Most certainly the "Hunter

Orange" attire, which was required in my home state, had to go . . . the Alaskan outfitter I spoke with said emphatically: "Don't show up with orange hunting clothes!" . . . Heck, mine was all orange.

In most mid west and eastern states, hunters are required to wear some bright orange hunting attire primarily for safety reasons (so you don't get mistakenly shot by another hunter). Hunters have also been told by state game authorities that deer and other animals cannot see or detect color. Consequently, hunters need not be concerned about the legal requirements to wear a minimum of a bright orange vest (not to mention the stiff financial penalties if you elected not to wear it). This color blindness advise had scientific support since most animals cannot detect color the same as humans. However, I believed then, and now, that deer (and other animals) can clearly detect differences in hues. In reality, wearing hunter orange made you stand out like a sore thumb in the woods to both hunters and the hunted. If you went deer hunting covered in bright orange attire you might as well put a blinking light on the top of your head and then go crashing through the woods honking a horn like Clarabelle the clown. Bright orange was a dead giveaway in the woods.

Acquiring new camping and hunting gear required numerous (and sometimes expensive) trips to the outdoor sports stores. One trip to a newly opened sporting goods store proved to be somewhat amusing. My purchases on this day only totaled $18.88, as I was primarily there to do some price shopping for the expensive stuff. On totaling my purchases (aiming the bar-code reader), the cashier, who was much younger than I, said "Oh, 1888, that was certainly a good year!"

I thought for a moment and said, "Let's see in 1888, the Civil War was over, I believe Cleveland was our president; what exactly happened that made 1888 a good year?"

The casher responded saying, "Oh, I don't know; I was never very good at geography." No wonder I worry about our public education system letting us down.

On another visit to a larger retail outdoor/sporting goods store, I was shopping at the back of the store, and a very helpful clerk took care of my purchase, saving me the wait in a long line that had formed at the store's front checkout stations. The item I purchased was large and did not fit into a store shopping bag, so the clerk said she would tag it for me and promptly placed a sticker on the box, writing across the sticker "paided." Heck, even I knew that the word was spelled payd, or is that paid? No matter, I got my gear.

My guide's gear restriction was very specific due to the distances involved with this hunt's aircraft weight limits and requirements for the pack animals. The primary restriction limited me to bringing only two waterproof bags, totaling thirty-five pounds each to carry all my gear, guns, ammunition, camping equipment, boots, and clothes. Holy Toledo, it would be a major challenge for me to get my gear down to seventy pounds to fit into two waterproof bags (another goal).

Preparation Of Hunting Rifle

"Don't use a cannon to shoot a sparrow."

Chinese Proverb

This part of my preparation started out easily as I only had one reliable rifle of sufficient caliber to hunt moose. Interestingly, I purchased the rifle in 1965 specifically to hunt large game, including a moose in Alaska. I was a nineteen-year-old soldier serving in the U.S. Army in what was then, West Germany and little did I know that it would be another forty years before I would finally realize that dream of a moose hunt.

My "moose gun" was a British-made Parker Hale, Super Safari Rifle of 30-06 caliber. I had used this rifle to successfully hunt white tail deer in Pennsylvania. However a one-hundred-fifty-pound deer was of significantly smaller stature than a sixteen hundred pound bull moose.

Bullet nomenclature varied and the terminology employed to identify various cartridges was inconsistent. However the reference to a 30-06 caliber cartridge simply meant a 30 caliber (diameter of the round in thousandths of an inch) that was designed in the year 1906, and was one of the few bullets identified in this diameter/date manner. It was the standard military rifle cartridge used by the United States through World War I, World War II, and Korea and is still a popular cartridge used by hunters because it has wide range hunting capabilities. Bullet ballistics for the 30-06 cartridge using a 180 grain projectile showed that the 30-06 has a muzzle velocity of 2700 feet/second with measured muzzle energy of 2914 foot/pounds. Most big game hunters considered a cartridge with a muzzle velocity of at least 3000 feet/second and muzzle energy of at least 3600 foot pounds to be the minimum cartridge needed for hunting moose because an Alaskan Moose was such a large game animal. While the 30-06 caliber cartridge was no cannon and might be on the light end for a moose gun, even for the Chinese, I was confident that in the hands of a competent hunter (me) and sighted in to hit precisely two inches high at one-hundred yards that it would perform just fine out to three-hundred yards. Beyond three-hundred yards, with adverse winds, a hunter using the 30-06 would rely too much on luck for accuracy. Consequently I planed to pass on any shooting opportunity that was beyond three-hundred yards (This plan would later change when confronted with a three-hundred plus yard shot facing a direct headwind).

Complications arose when I found that I needed to replace the telescopic sights. European made rifles of the mid 1960s had a unique sight mounting arrangement that required me to invest a considerable amount of time and energy into the mounting configuration before the installation of my new telescopic sights was completed. Once this was finished the sighting in process began - an important step. I wanted to have 100% confidence in my rifle's accuracy before the start of my hunt. It would not be a good idea to be firing wildly, off target, through the air when the game animal you seek is so difficult to locate and my hunting time in the Alaska range of mountains might only yield a single shooting opportunity.

It had been years since I used my deer (now moose) rifle, therefore I scheduled plenty of time at the rifle range to regain my proficiency with the 30-06 (another goal). On one cold wet and rainy day I decided to do some shooting at the rifle range to see how the rifle (and I at sixty-one) operated in adverse weather. I knew, first hand, that in Alaska adverse weather could arrive at any time and linger for days. On this particular day only two other people were at the range, and for safety we coordinated our firing activity. Both individuals were very pleasant young men. One was shooting rifled slugs from a scoped twelve gauge shotgun and having a difficult time. He was shooting wildly and barely able to hold his gun steady enough to even hit anywhere on the target at one-hundred yards. The second young man was shooting with exceptional accuracy using a 7 MM rifle, and my all time favorite military rifle, the M-1 Garand also of 30-06 caliber. You see, the M-1 Garand was the rifle I used to qualify as an expert marksman in Army boot camp. When my shooting was finished I started using my sixty power spotting scope to help the second shooter by calling his three shot groups at one hundred yards. To secure accuracy, a shooter needed to fire three rounds and then check to see where those rounds hit the target before making any sight adjustments. The sixty power magnification of the spotting scope made bullet strikes on the target visible at one-hundred yards. As a result, the shooter did not need to walk the distance to the target to find out where his three shot groups hit. All I could see through my spotting scope on his targets were three shot groups that appeared to be single holes dead center. As a marksman this kid was absolutely excellent and without a doubt, he was one of the most accurate shooters I had ever met. As we talked, I also found out that he was home on leave from the U.S. Army, his unit was the 101st Airborne Division, and he would return to the war in Iraq in two weeks. Sometimes preparation took on a much deeper meaning and for this young man shooting accuracy clearly held a high level of importance.

I had a somewhat bizarre experience happen once at work regarding shooting accuracy. At the time this happened, I was the plant personnel manager at a unionized shop and had to call in an employee for a disciplinary meeting (now referred to as a behavior modification meeting). This particular individual was not new to the disciplinary process due to his bad habit of not showing up for work and arriving late when he did appear. Sadly, he had not modified his behavior following a multitude of meetings and disciplinary suspensions. We had reached the end of the trail. The disciplinary, or behavior modification process, reached the final stage called "Suspension preliminary to discharge," and this worker's actions left no alternative other than discharge. I must add that discharge decisions in an industrial setting can never be taken lightly as termination from employment is tantamount to corporate capital punishment. With that said this guy had pushed well past the limits of reason.

As a side note, it seemed absurd to issue work suspensions for an absentee worker (almost a reward), but like it or not, that's the way the system works when behavior is not modified. What I found truly bizarre in this meeting was the employee's excuse for being tardy. He was very upset with me when I informed him that I intended to proceed with the conversion to discharge even after he explained that he had a very good reason for being late (for the zillionth time). This character said, and I believe this to be true, that he was going through his house shooting rats with a rifle, and he accidentally shot the alarm clock in his bedroom! How could I possibly expect him to arrive at work when his alarm clock had been shot? Wow, I thought I'd heard all the excuses for being late, but this one was a first. Unfortunately, for this employee the rat shooting dilemma didn't override his well established poor work record and accordingly his suspension was converted to discharge. Discharging characters like this lost soul will always cause HR people to hesitate, look around and think about the post office as they walk into the parking lot at the end of a long day.

I have heard many weird reasons given for reporting off work. However my last boss enjoyed reminding me that I was the one who called in with the weirdest work report-off that he ever heard in his entire career. This happened in August of 1992. I was on a solo exploration adventure in Alaska and called to tell him that I would be unable to make it back to work on time because I was pinned down by an erupting volcano. True story, it was August 18, 1992, to be exact, the volcano was Mount Spurr, and the call to him was actually made by my wife after I was able to reach her to say that I was fine but would experience a truly unavoidable delay. At the time I was upset about getting caught in the wrath of Mount Spurr, but as I look back on it, the experience was monumental. It was exciting and exhilarating watching the sky darken as the gigantic black cloud rose thousands of feet into the air, then drifted overhead, completely blocking out the sun, casting fear on everyone below, and then for hours fine volcanic ash rained down. I was standing in a rainstorm of dirt, absolutely unbelievable but true. I keep a souvenir jar of that volcanic ash in my den and remember the experience vividly to this day.

To me that eruption of Mount Spurr was an unmistakable reminder that humans do not control the earth; it is the earth that decides what to do and when it will be done.

This exploratory adventure into the Alaska wilds served to reinforce my desire to be thorough in preparing for this next journey. Time was available and everything had to be meticulously planned, including my transportation.

TRANSPORTATION PREPARATION

The vehicle I chose for my Alaska journey was my five-year-old Toyota Avalon that had operated flawlessly for over 73,000 miles. The car was a four-door sedan, built low to the ground, powered by a very smooth and economical V-6 engine with a trunk that had adequate storage capacity for the camping and hunting gear I planned to take. Now if you listened to some of the old-road veterans who had driven north and crossed the Alcan highway, they would tell you that my choice of vehicle was 100% wrong, and the four-door sedan could not possibly hold up to the rigors of travel to Alaska over the Alcan highway. They would advise that the ruggedness of the road north required, at a minimum, a sturdy four-wheel-drive vehicle with high ground clearance and protective skid plates below the engine. The vehicle would also need radiator guards, headlight guards, extra spare tires, spare fuel cans, and a ton of emergency rations. Taking in this rugged-vehicle, advise, it would have seemed clear that my sedan had no tough-car qualities and as vehicles went, could not be more opposite. Even my wife was convinced that

I would destroy the car before I ever reached Fairbanks (sometimes her confidence in me was not so great). Separate from this wealth of wrong vehicle information, I had occasion to meet with travelers who recently crossed the Alcan and was advised by them that most, or all, of the highway had been paved. I concluded that my sedan would do very well on this journey.

I planned to take time to assure that all maintenance matters would be addressed and my car would be in top shape by departure time. I also understood that the journey could be a monumental undertaking for both the old car and the old driver. Hey, that would be part of the challenge for this new adventure.

My plan for the solo drive north to Fairbanks, Alaska, to hunt a moose was not viewed with favor by a single person I know. Orion may have liked my idea because he, by myth, was a gifted hunter and enjoyed hunting in any form, but from family and friends the feedback received ran from "You are crazy" to "You'll never make it alone." Not a single word of encouragement came my way, which partially, maybe ironically, reinforced my desire to launch the journey north and prove to myself that I could do it. Then, with the confidence of a Daniel Boone, I simply continued with my preparations.

My hand-held global positioning system (GPS) informed me that the distance (straight line) from my house to the house of an old US Army friend living in Fairbanks, Alaska, was 3003 miles. The American Automobile Association (AAA) who planned my ground route advised that the driving distance would total 3880 miles. The most direct route was my return drive home that included two road repair detours of approximately twelve miles. This return drive proved the AAA's estimate to be very accurate. The planned journey definitely represented a lot of solo driving, and I did take time to give considerable thought to the advice of a few nay-sayers before I completely dismissed their negative input. What would it be like to cross this great distance, travel through Canada, cross the Rockies where there would be narrow roads, steep drop-offs and no guard rails? Those questions actually only intensified the challenge.

CHAPTER 3

A GOOD GUIDE
(REFLECTIONS ON LEADERSHIP)

Regulations in Alaska required that in many of Alaska's game management areas, non-resident and foreign hunters use a licensed and registered Alaska Hunting Guide. It was interesting to read in the regulations that the Alaska Department of Fish and Game (ADF&G) referred to any hunters or potential hunters who were not legal residents of Alaska as "aliens." I found the ADF&G to be a pretty thorough organization and I had to guess that the alien terminology was placed into the law to make sure they covered anyone traveling from places like Ohio, Florida, Japan or even Mars. Some hunters were offended by the requirement to use a guide, even though a good one is critical when you hunt in a distant area that is unfamiliar and harbors potential life threatening danger in the form of terrain, weather, and apex predators. Like it or not, the requirement was written into law. It was also important to keep in mind that the hunting guide business in Alaska was (and remains) a very important component of the state's economy and many of the big game guides worked closely with the ADF&G supporting game conservation programs. Clearly, the ADF&G recognizes value in setting up programs to license and register hunting guides.

WHAT IS A GUIDE?

Let me give you an example of just how important guides can be to all of us. In my job, I was called on periodically to present supervisor and manager-skills training seminars. At the beginning of each seminar, I reminded everyone in the class that they were successful individuals and successful professionals, and I meant that as a very true statement. Every single one of them had succeeded in school, in college, in their personal lives, and in their vocation. They were not selected to be in the training class because they were not successful; it was just the opposite. I then asked them a few questions.

First, I asked them to think about and write down names of two or three people they admired and who had personally helped them succeed. For instance, professional people like engineers or scientists told me often that it was a teacher who helped and inspired them to get started in their career. In some situations they described themselves as absolute failures in school until Ms. So-n-so called them aside to talk to them about what they were capable of doing. Parents also surfaced as motivational examples in meetings I held, and parents are true models of tenacity when it comes to follow-up. Past managers or supervisors were mentioned in every single meeting as examples of the people who inspirationally helped them the most and the ones that they genuinely admired. That claim may sound unrealistic in today's world where "boss bashing" seems to be so popular, but it is true that a worker's supervisor, in any line of work, can be a very positive force in that individual's life. Other relatives were named and given credit for their inspiration: Grandparents, stepparents, uncles, aunts, siblings, and in one meeting a guy actually told me it was a past HR Director that he worked with. I was the HR Director for this company at the time and was sure that I was in for some real BS from this class participant. Later though, when he answered the second question, it was clear that he was serious.

I asked for some participants to share the names they had and then listed those names and/or titles on one column on a board at the front of the class and then . . .

Second, I asked them what exactly was it that these people did that inspired and helped them to succeed. In the HR Directors case, he was consistently doing those little things that so often prove to be critically important: remembering names, remembering to follow up on questions asked, remembering to provide positive reinforcement for work completed, remembering to say hello, and remembering to focus on the positive.

In these training seminars I got positive responses 100% of the time to my second question such as: "He or she listened", "They took time for me", "They showed me how to do it", "They explained things", "They cared", "They set the right example", "They encouraged me", "They were empathetic," and "were patient". Patience almost always came up and without question is one of the most important components of leadership. I can also tell you with absolute truth that every action the participants described fit right into the leadership training program that followed, and all I needed to do throughout my training seminar was reinforce these leadership examples that the participants gave me in the beginning.

I listed the various actions taken on the board in a second column next to the names I had been given and then . . . (3)

Third, I asked the participants about the outcome of the actions taken by the people they named. Here, the answers reflected the accomplishments that each individual in the seminar was so proud of: "I went on to college," "I landed a new job," "I got my college degree," "I got a promotion'" "I made my life better," "I became a better person," "a better parent" . . . the list was long and so very positive.

When this list was posted to the board, I reminded the meeting participants that the people they named who had helped them succeed did not hold their hand going forward. The teacher that inspired the engineer did not go on to college with that person so that she could do the homework or take tests for him. No, in each and every case the person they named saw the need, took action, got results, and moved on. They were very results-oriented individuals, not wishy-washy do-gooders; they took action and got results . . . just like everyone in supervision and management needed to do.

The managers and supervisors who were named as being inspirational in these meetings were not named because they were extra generous with pay increases or that they consistently handed the person the easiest work assignments. No, in fact the exact opposite was often times the case. They were held in the highest regard because they cared to do their job right, and they cared about those who worked for them. They listened, they were supportive, they were patient, they asked for help, they established expectations, they were results oriented and yes, they were guides.

Leaders have two important characteristics: First, they're going somewhere; second, they're able to persuade other people to go along with them. Good guides make great leaders.

In my personal life I was fortunate to have some great supervisors, Joe Huss and Jim Rimmel were two and are both referred to later in this book. There was a third guy who I need to mention along with

Joe and Jim and his name was Mike Luther. Mike may well rank at the top of my list of inspirational supervisors and influential people and it is not because working for him was a piece of cake. Mike was brilliant and able to solve complex business and people issues with incredible ease. I saw Mike assemble detailed plans off the top of his head, plans that would take most business leaders weeks to study and prepare. His brilliance alone made him a tough guy to keep up with as his expectations were anything but mediocre, and the job I held at the time was one that could easily turn into a living monster that would eat you alive. When I had occasion to talk to Mike about any trouble I had keeping up with my workload he would, half joking, say things like: "Remember Bill, everyday has twenty-four hours." Mike had his own way of setting high expectations.

At that time I also attended graduate school in the evenings, working toward an MBA and taking a full academic load. I was already knocking on the door of that twenty-four-hour day and struggling to keep up with my work, so you might ask why would I put Mike at the top of my list? Mike would be there for two reasons, first I learned more about management and the HR discipline from Mike in the three years that I worked for him than I have learned from anyone else in my professional career, and second, like Joe Huss and Jim Rimmel, he genuinely cared about me and my career development. Mike was a good person and mentally a light year ahead of the professors I had in my MBA program. Working for Mike Luther was a rewarding and unparalleled learning experience.

My three question "who helped you succeed" exercise was always an eye-opener and a great way to get people involved at the start of a leadership seminar. I would ask a final question, and did not ask this question looking for an open answer. I asked them: "Did you ever go back to this person and say thanks?" Not the "Oh yeah, thanks" line, but a very sincere thank you. "Thank You Mr. or Ms. So-n-so for doing (specifically what they did) that helped me so much and because of your help I was able to (specifically what you accomplished), and I sincerely appreciate the things you did for me." I stopped asking for a response to that question because the answers came back too often in two negative forms. First as "No" (sad) and then sometimes with the qualifier: "No, but now it's too late" (even more sad).

As you read this right now stop. Stop to think about those individuals who helped you succeed in life, and write down their names and what they did for you. If you have never thanked them, verbally or in writing, do so now before it is too late. You will feel very good about doing it, and the person will genuinely appreciate every word you say or write.

HUNTING AND GUIDING

The point of my story about past training seminars should be clear: People who inspired and helped these individuals succeed were both hunters and guides. They found (with hunting skill) an opportunity, they took action (were guides), and they got results. Good leaders are hunters. Good leaders are guides.

Let me give you another example of a hunter/guide that we can all relate to, and know well. That hunter/guide is your family doctor. Your family doctor has to hunt constantly seeking information to determine what medical problem exists, what caused it to happen and what to prescribe as a cure. Upon completion of the hunt the physician then serves as your guide to implement corrective treatment and/or action. My family doctor is an MD named Marvin Feldstein, and he is one of the best hunter/guides I have ever met in my life, yet I don't know that he ever set foot in the woods with rifle in hand hunting wild game. He is good because he continually cultivates his hunting skills and commands respect as a people-guide. Fortunately, family physicians make the best people managers.

I wrote thousands of job descriptions throughout my career and cannot name a single position that didn't require hunting and guiding skills. For businesses to operate effectively, managers need to hunt using statistical process control, computer analysis, interviewing, or whatever means is available that enables them to make decisions and take action, be guides for products and/or services to customers.

In life and in business we are all hunters, it is human nature, and our hunting activity will certainly provide us with opportunities to serve as guides. Whenever you identify that need to serve as a guide for any individual(s) working for or with you, accept it and use it wisely. It may prove to be a very golden opportunity yielding lifetime results.

ALASKA HUNTING GUIDE

I started my search for an Alaska hunting guide with online advice from a number of sources including the ADF&G. One of my online resources implied that the ADF&G was not doing a very good job of qualifying and monitoring registered guides (that is determining a guide's knowledge, experience and qualifications). This source went on to say that hunters needed to take time and be cautious in selecting hunting guides because with ADF&G qualified guides "for every good guide there are three bad ones." Most (actually all) experienced hunters I met in Alaska corroborated that dismal three to one ratio. Keep in mind that the ADF&G working with the Alaska Department of Commerce has control over and responsibility for establishing guide qualifications, guide registration, and guide licensing. Now think about this: Can you possibly imagine being engaged in a manufacturing operation with your quality control department telling you that statistically your current product quality level is only twenty-five percent? Crazy! Forget six sigma! In manufacturing our quality goal was always targeted at "six sigma" as a unit of measure for the integrity of products we made. Put simply, a six sigma quality means that all products that you manufacture must be measured for fitness to standard and recorded. These measurements are graphed, and over time this graph will reflect a normal bell curve configuration. Under the guidelines of six sigma the acceptable quality for the products made must fit on this graph within six standard deviations of the mean. Six standard deviations translates into an acceptable quality rate that only allows three bad parts per million.

In manufacturing you made high quality parts to assure safety, preserve the integrity of the process and keep customers happy. Similar, albeit different, quality requirements should exist for government agencies, and in this case, high quality guides are needed to insure safety, preserve the integrity of the system and keep customers (hunters/taxpayers) happy.

Think about and compare the manufacturing quality standard I just described to guide quality standards that appear to be accepted by the ADF&G. Six sigma equals three bad parts per million and three out of four converts to 750,000 bad parts (guides) per million! If what I've been told is true about guide qualification standards, the ADF&G has a lot of work to do." I mention this hunting guide quality concern because later in my journey I found ample cause for complaint.

Guides are important, very important. In chapter ten I'll share with you a dramatic, life-threatening example of guide failure.

Using the recommendation of a friend I contacted an Alaska guide (outfitter) service that operates in central Alaska and establishes guided hunts in the very area where I wanted to hunt. My friend had hunted with this guide on several occasions and gave him an unqualified excellent recommendation. Eventually I completed arrangements with this outfitter to support the hunting part of my journey.

CHAPTER 4

TRAVEL BEGINS
(COMPONENTS OF PERFORMANCE EVALUATIONS)

"Even if you're on the right track.
you'll get run over if you just sit there."

Will Rogers

Normal, Illinois, was not directly on my route to Alaska. However, just saying that city name had always raised my level of curiosity. Just who pray tell would live in a place called "Normal?" Could this be the home of the average person we referenced so often in school and business? The average person who is identified on every business employee performance appraisal form (they rest in middle of the performance evaluation continuum), referenced despairingly in every employee motivation/training program, and the key person used in establishing all human performance "norms." Traveling through "Normal" could provide a unique opportunity to meet some truly average (normal) people and I simply couldn't pass it by.

I say this because throughout my working life I found that no one ever claimed to be just normal. Normal is only average, and introspectively, everyone sees themselves in a more positive light. Most people feel insulted if they are labeled as average because in our society, we have been taught to believe that being just average is unacceptable. Through social practice, "average" ends up being a term only applied to that other person, not me!

Think about this. Back in the 1950s and 1960s, many school systems in the country religiously gave out Intelligence Quotient (IQ) tests to every kid in school, and a test score of 100 was determined to be the quantitative equivalent of average (dead center on the bell curve). I have to ask that if you also participated in these IQ tests, did you ever hear a kid in your class boast about a score of 100? Certainly no kid ever volunteered to report that they were measured below 100, and when asked, almost everyone inflated their IQ score number to around 114. Being average on an IQ Test (100) was just deemed unacceptable by parents, teachers, and students alike. IQ scores were also a handy (and poor) tool that some teachers used to categorize students as academic winners or losers, those who would do well in class and those who would not were often predetermined. Sadly, a student could fail a course before they ever set foot into the classroom. Being measured as a failure isn't anything anyone desires and consequently a score in the range of 114 was a common claim from most kids who may have been measured in the average range on those IQ tests.

With IQ scores, I suspect that if you inflated (fabricated) your score to above 120, you might be expected to say something clever in your response, but if your score was low and you inflated it to near 114, then you were relatively safe. In a way, through practice, 114 became everyone's acceptable average. Back in my school days, academic behaviorists didn't really understand what the Pygmalion effect was, so educators just called (branded) people as stupid or smart based on these IQ tests and didn't think anything of it. Today, most educators do understand the far reaching effects of negative reinforcement. Behavior studies have shown time and again that if a young person is labeled stupid and called stupid by teachers, peers or other influential people that he or she is condemned to respond in kind, believing that he or she is genuinely stupid, true or not. Studies have also shown that once this negative conditioning takes place, it is difficult if not impossible, to reverse. Positive reinforcement consistently yields the best results in school, in sports, and in business.

Another very interesting phenomenon in the work setting is that no managers ever seem to have average workers in their departments. Certainly not average when viewing the performance evaluations that managers complete for their workers. Those performance evaluations always seem to be skewed to the right side (high performance side) of the normal bell curve. There is a reason for this, of course, and that is any pay increase a manager is permitted to give to a worker is conditioned and supported by that worker's performance evaluation, and an average evaluation provides only mediocre or no pay adjustments (you see, average is not good). Here too is where that average person ends up getting an official score from his/her supervisor of 114 and in so doing the manager avoids the painful task of telling the subordinate the truth, and the truth may be that his or her work performance hovers at below average.

Over the years managers consistently reported to me that the other departments were stuffed with average people but definitely not theirs, and it was not fair that they should be held to the same wage controls. The manager would insist that his/her department was better, it was special and clearly operating above the company average (in the 114 range, I assume). That is, everyone in the manager's department was an above average or superior worker until the manager decided that he/she must terminate that person's employment (for bad work performance, of course). It was at this time that the HR person (me) refused to allow the termination to take place because the department manager had evaluated the "to-be-terminated" worker consistently as an excellent worker, well above average and hardly a candidate for a performance termination. I saw this scenario unfold numerous times in my career and it always drove me nuts. In this type of situation the manager was then told that he/she needed to engage in some behavior modification (actually for the manager as well as the worker) and if improved work performance did not materialize, then the manager was obligated to start building a case against the employee that reflected the individual's sub-par performance combined with documented opportunities given for improvement (actions that should have transpired in the first place). The good news was that generally once any individual heard the truth about his or her work (and more importantly what was expected from them), he or she shaped up (modified behavior) and any perceived performance problem simply went away.

I can also tell you that without responsible HR intervention, a conversion to discharge, in a situation like this can be costly. The Equal Employment Opportunity Commission (EEOC) looks at the termination scenario with a jaundiced eye anytime they are confronted with this type of complaint. The EEOC refers to these above average/ superior worker discharge situations as "the fast down-hillers" and will, rightfully, question how management evaluations on the aggrieved employee went from years of excellence to a sudden surge of below average performance and rapid termination. Executive and managerial actions can often be very difficult to defend, and the legal vindication of the fast down hillers is generally painful and expensive.

Formal performance evaluations need to be consistent, objective, and free of bias from non-work related issues or legally protected status.

A major corporation in Youngstown, Ohio, lost a twelve million dollar class-action lawsuit based almost exclusively on poorly completed performance appraisals. This company unwisely made the mistake of abrasively terminating their HR Director, who was quick to point out his above average and superior evaluations to a plaintiff attorney. This lawyer was clever enough to subpoena all the performance appraisals of those individuals at the company that the plaintiff's lawyer determined to have been affected (legally defined as affected-class) then easily tied those performance appraisal documents into some age discrimination "legalese" language. Bingo, his case was made. This company, unwittingly, put the hangman's noose around its own neck (more on this subject matter in chapter fifteen).

So here's my point. If no kids in the schools I've attended claim to be average, no people in the businesses where I've worked these many years claim to be average, and no business managers claim to have average people working for them, then just who is this average person and where the Sam-hill does he/she live and work?

Trying to answer that question is what took me on a visit to Normal, Illinois. My guess was that discovering where average folks live was much more likely in Normal than it would be in abnormal cities like perhaps Los Angeles, San Francisco, or New York. Mr. & Ms. Average just might be living in Normal doing average things, having average families, getting average pay increases, and enjoying life smack dab in the middle of the normal bell curve.

NORMAL, ILLINOIS

Driving to Normal took me off course in relation to my moose hunt. The first four hours or so of driving covered just over two hundred miles and yet my GPS indicated that I was twenty-four miles farther away from Fairbanks. Christopher Columbus planned to reach the East by sailing west, but I did not plan to reach the North by sailing south. Consequently, I became very anxious to see Normal and get back on track heading north.

Normal looked, well, normal. It had normal streets, normal cops, normal pedestrians, and the people I talked to all seemed to be very normal, absent of a couple young people with orange and green hair that I saw standing near a bookstore in town. There was an interesting welcome sign that I saw while driving into the city with a large plaque commemorating a Normal resident named Kirstin Thompson who won the state discus championship. With no disrespect to Kirsten it seemed to me that a city of 45,400 residents would have been able to muster something else to this accomplishment . . . maybe an academic decathlon victory, a state spelling bee winner, or a Nobel Prize.

It turned out that Normal is also the home of Illinois State University (ISU). ISU is certainly a large and a fine academic institution plus the draw of college students and teaching faculty into this area (as a percent of the total population) must have a positive influence on IQ test scores. The legitimate average IQ score in Normal may actually be 114. Statisticians will remind you that half the people you know are below average, but I doubt that this belief holds true in Normal. Normal-Normal, Illinois, students sitting in the high school cafeteria discussing IQ test results probably inflate the number to well over 120. So, if the city's average IQ score is at or over 114, then it is unlikely that there are many people living in Normal of average intelligence, average ability, or average anything. My detoured drive left that question unanswered. The drive to Normal appeared to be an investigative failure.

You know, I still have to wonder if employers in Normal do as crummy of a job as is done elsewhere when it comes to completing performance appraisals correctly. It would be interesting to see if, on average, a higher IQ leads to more consistent and accurate feedback regarding work performance. I'm dubious as there is no guarantee that brains and courage coincide, and it takes a recognizable degree of courage for a supervisor, at any level of an organization, to complete and present an honest or fair performance appraisal.

In some ways, we are all average, and we are all above and below average. Each person has abilities, weaknesses, and strengths, and we all have our own genius. We are smart about different things in different ways, be it scientific theory, medical research, baseball statistics, NASCAR history, or whatever. My father once advised me that it is not a good idea to put oneself above others. He said, and it is true, that a person can learn something from anyone; even a bum on the street knows things that others do not. Some of what the bum knows might even rest at the very cradle of life; who are we, where are we going, why are we here, what obligations do we have to help one another.

I truly believe that buried inside each person on earth rests tremendous potential in two key forms. The first form is a potential to accomplish things beyond our existing imagination. Albert Einstein was quoted as saying "Imagination is more important than knowledge." He was so right, and we need to imagine more to grow, and we need to imagine more to learn, as no single person on earth has ever fully employed 100% of the physical or mental capabilities each possesses. The second form resting inside every soul is the potential for kindness and generosity toward other humans. Humans evolved on earth with the power to reason and also with the potential to care. How great it would be if we could get all political, and certainly religious leaders, throughout the world to put their imaginations to work developing this second internal human form.

My visit to Normal was brief and while it was certainly interesting to tour this city and the university campus, it did not provide a tremendous amount of enlightenment, nothing bad and yet nothing exceptionally fascinating from a human behavior standpoint. The time spent in Normal provided an opportunity to give more thought to average and average performance in work and life. What I realized is that we all operate in the middle range of that bell curve in most of what we do each and every day, so being average isn't such a bad thing after all. I think good business leaders (guides) need to do a better job of recognizing average performance. Leaders need to better appreciate this given and provide a form of recognition for those who, on average, are always at work and always getting their jobs completed on time. Without some appreciation for middle of the bell curve work performance, the work performance will only gravitate lower skewing the bell curve to the left. Positive recognition and appreciation for average work performance can only enrich performance results skewing the bell curve to the right where most of us, introspectively, think we reside. In management, do not forget average people and remember that in many respects we are all average.

In graduate school one of my better professors had a sign on his office wall (amid a cluster of others) that read: "Remember to take care of your 'C' students . . . they are the ones who come back with the big endowments." A truism of sorts as those average Joe's are the ones who often cope with change best and are able to implement new ideas by selling and negotiating (hunt and guide) within their organization.

It was time to say good-bye to Normal, shift gears, and make a mad dash to British Columbia and the starting point of my long-awaited drive along the famous Alcan highway. This would be one mammoth mad dash too, as it would take three or four days of heads-up driving.

Chapter 5

Mad Dash
to the Boreal Forests
(Thoughts on jobs
and people at work)

A mad dash through Illinois, Wisconsin, North Dakota, Saskatchewan, Alberta, and into British Columbia was a significant undertaking that consumed time and energy, not to mention money, as gas in some parts of Canada climbed above the $1.30 CN per liter ($5.00/U.S. gallon) level.

Wisconsin was beautiful and my overnight stay in the area known as "The Dells" was incredibly refreshing. The lakes and geography of the Dells were formed by the last ice age and were an awesome sight. I arrived late in the day, yet even with the fading sunlight, I saw impressive water-filled arenas of beauty. My short stay proved to be an enjoyable learning experience primarily because the outdoor sites were so spectacular. Within that learning interlude I discovered that The Dells could also be expensive (not too enjoyable). The tourist season had not ended, so room rates remained sky high. Dinner at a restaurant cost twice what I expected, service was slow, and gas prices were the highest I had seen yet on the journey, they would get higher as I moved north.

I had time during my Wisconsin visit to reflect back on a prior business trip to the city of Waukesha, Wisconsin near Milwaukee. On my last day, I finished early and being an airplane buff, decided to visit a small local airport to see what types of general aviation airplanes might be on the field. As it turned out, Waukesha was the home base for a relatively large number of general aviation airplanes. Most airplanes were in closed hangers but dozens were tied down on the tarmac outside the hangers. The airplanes secured outside were of all types and interesting to examine up close. While on the airfield, I saw a car drive up and park near one of the tied down airplanes.

This particular airplane, called an Ercoupe, was one that had become a relatively rare flying machine. Ercoupes (later called the Alon Aircoupe and then Mooney M10 Cadet) were first made before World War II and designed with coordinated flight controls. In other words, the pilot had a steering yoke that would operate, or coordinate, the rudders and ailerons simultaneously. It was a two-seat, side-by-side, low-wing airplane with a very distinctive twin rudder/vertical stabilizer arrangement. I had never flown one but always looked upon them as aerodynamically distinctive and beautiful flying machines. Other pilots had told me that they were generally an easy airplane to fly, just a little lethargic and could be a real handful if you were landing on a runway with a strong cross-wind (then coordinated controls became a detriment).

Here is what I found most interesting. It turned out the driver of the car was wheelchair bound. He was a very cheerful and friendly person, who I initially thought was there to get a ride in an airplane. Not so. He started around the Ercoupe in his wheelchair untied the ropes that secured the plane in place and doing a pre-flight inspection. I immediately went over to offer my assistance and he said, "Oh no, I can do just fine, watch me!"

We talked briefly as he did his pre-flight check of the airplane: wheels, brakes, ailerons, rudders, propeller, and engine check, including oil level, a procedure that required him to pull up out of the chair above the engine nacle. He moved to the port-side wing of the plane, at the rear near the wing root, and pulled himself up onto the wing, reached down and folded his wheelchair up, placed it on its side, slid back the cockpit canopy, and got into the plane. After completing his initial cockpit checks, he called out "clear prop," engaged the starter, and watched his control panel as the airplane's engine gauges came to life, and the Ercoupe began to warm up. He then taxied to the "run-up" pad at the end of the runway to complete his final flight control and engine checks before flight. As he advanced the throttle and the Ercoupe began to move, I started to wave good-bye and then thought no, not good enough. I snapped to attention and gave this pilot a sharp military salute. He smiled, returned my salute and was on his way. What a remarkable individual.

When he lifted off the runway my heart, mind, and soul was with him in the cockpit. For any pilot, solo flight take offs are special and exhilarating. He lined up in the center of the runway, advanced the throttle, and accelerated forward. Then his flight controls began to firm up, he pulled back on the yoke, and the airplane broke loose from the bonds of gravity - - he was airborne. The pilot relaxed, isolated and detached from earth's activities and in his own little world. As I watched this pilot climb away from the airfield in his Ercoupe, I knew that his personal little world was a very special one. He was doing just fine as he stated.

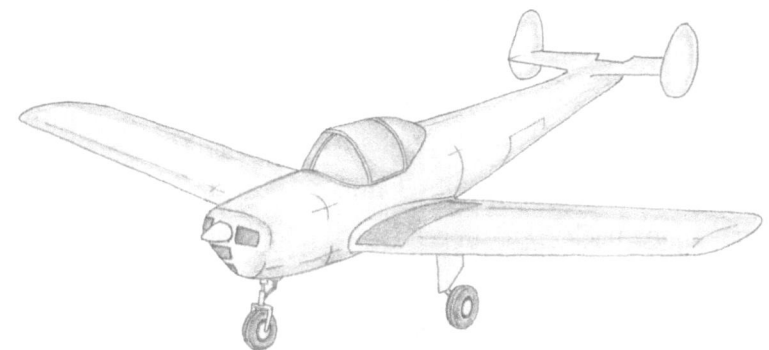

Ercoupe – aerodynamically distinctive

This pilot story is included here because it stands out as a classic example of a person with a very positive can-do attitude. To quote Henry Ford: "If you think you can . . . you're right."

Later, in chapter fifteen, I talk more about physically disabled workers and what an important, highly productive, human asset they can be in any business.

On this journey through Wisconsin my learning experiences continued as I also learned that they had major thunderstorms. When I was leaving the Dells in the early morning, there were thunderstorms with major lightning activity all around me, but I seemed to be driving in a "no-rain zone." It was breathtaking to see the continuous bolts of lightning striking out all around me. One major storm close by and directly to my south had rain so heavy that it looked like a solid black cloud all the way to the earth's surface.

Weather storms have always fascinated and intrigued me, and this unique early morning drive through the powerful thunderstorms surrounding me, including the darkness of the massive cloud structure to my south, was positively captivating.

The no-rain zone seemed to personify my journey north as well as my position in life. I was experiencing freedom in a way that I have never felt before. This experience was not a temporary break with reality and a return to the past. On this journey the past was gone. The chaos surrounded me --- it did not matter; my new journey was well underway.

Entering Minnesota, the rains subsided, and the sky opened up to a clear blue. This state also held tremendously beautiful outdoor views, and it was hard to keep focused on the road with so many things to see in the woods, hills, and farms. I had past work assignments in Minnesota and always managed to find time to see some of the many lakes that gave Minnesota its special recognition for beauty. Unfortunately, as a business manager, I had also found the state's employment and labor laws to be a little expensive and unkind toward employers. This state maintained very liberal interpretations on labor legal matters like Workers Compensation, and that "give-away" mentality always drove down productivity at the same time it increased manufacturing costs. It could be a tough state to do business in, but then didn't Minnesota elect a pro-wrestler to the governor's office? With a tough guy like Jessie (the body) Ventura at the helm, you had to expect a few take-downs.

Well, despite the employment practice costs in Minnesota, I had to say that the landscape in this state was spectacular. Wildlife could be spotted throughout, and magnificent lakes were literally everywhere. In addition to their abundance, these lakes in Minnesota were utterly awe-inspiring.

Interesting too, as I was driving through Minnesota near route 94 and exit #100, I saw what appeared to be a large ranch right off to the west side of the highway with hundreds of majestic Elks. Elks are one of the large members of the deer family and I never identified them with the state of Minnesota. These bulls had impressive antlers that swept back over their body. The majority of this herd was clearly visible from route 94. At that time it was the being of the rutting season, and those bulls were proudly displaying their fully developed antlers, posturing for control of the herd. It was an impressive site to say the least.

Majestic North American Elk

Driving out of Minnesota into North Dakota the most impressive site to behold was a gigantic speed trap. I had never seen a speed trap orchestrated in such a forceful and systematic way. The North Dakota state police erected signs along route 94 just west of Fargo indicating that there was a construction zone ahead and a drop in speed of ten miles per hour. There actually wasn't any construction taking place, and the single traffic construction lane started at the base of a small hill that concealed the speed trap. The right lane was cordoned off by orange traffic cones (fake construction zone), and it was that lane where the state police were pulling over drivers at what had to be a record-breaking pace to issue citations. There were at least six police cars working this trap. They were writing citations as fast as their hands could go, so they could spin around on this highway (making illegal U-turns) to get their cars and radar guns back to the starting point at the base of the hill to highjack the next unsuspecting sucker. By any standards it was a speed trap free-for-all.

I did not get nabbed, but I did feel sorry for the line-up of poor unfortunate drivers getting citations, and I was sad too for law enforcement professionals everywhere. Speed traps like this one only served to tarnish the image of professional law enforcement.

Let me explain what I meant when I wrote "tarnished". Once, years ago, I attended an employment conference in Columbus, Ohio, where I met an individual who had an interesting and challenging management job. His responsibility was to find gainful and honest employment for convicts once they completed incarceration and were being released from custody at the Ohio State Penitentiary. I commented to him that his job had to be a very tough one - hunting jobs for those prisoners who had committed heinous crimes (Orion couldn't hunt down jobs for those lost souls). The manager told me that it was not as difficult as I might imagine. Ex-cons, including murderers, who had served their sentence, repented if you will, and truly seeking a fresh start in life were job candidates many employers would hire. He also told me that the most difficult ex-cons to find work for were the forgers, embezzlers, and other sneaky criminals. Through his experience he learned that "nobody trusts or will hire a sneaky son-of-a-gun." You see, they made themselves a tarnished employment commodity.

This North Dakota speed trap was sneaky - very sneaky - I didn't trust those guys.

On leaving Minot, North Dakota, for Canada in the early morning I was blessed to view a spectacular sky. It was a cool clear day, and the sun's early morning rays were streaking through a single cloud layer off to my east, creating beautiful colors of blues, reds, oranges, and grays. The farmers were already in the fields harvesting crops with those massive and impressive agricultural machines that attempt to fully automate the farming business. Still the sounds and fresh, fragrant smell of a Fall harvest was in the air and everywhere.

Even with highway construction taking place, it was a comfortable and relaxing drive north to the Canadian border.

CANADIAN CUSTOMS

At the Canadian border, I ran into a collection of the most unfriendly folks imaginable. You might think (as I did) that customs agents should be nice and pleasant. What I discovered was that being courteous was obviously not a job requirement for the characters on duty when I arrived, and the time taken to register my rifle and pay the twenty-five dollar fee (tax) proved to be an onerous burden.

As I watched these Canadian customs agents go about their work (or make an attempt to), I could not help but reflect on work in general and work's importance in the lives of most people. We identify with our work, we take ownership of our jobs, take pride in what we do and it is part of our daily conversation. Work has forever been part of who and what we are. We have always taken pride in belonging to the organization that held us in their employ.

The vast majority of people do want to work and be part of a bigger, more important endeavor. I saw and still see this even in individuals who are not happy in their jobs or particularly crazy about their employer. At times away from work when these people are asked, they respond readily with who they are, as a person, through their work and employer: "I'm important, not a no-body . . . I work at ABC Company, and I'm in the XYZ Department. I have significance, I am productive, and I am part of a more momentous endeavor." Work is important and it is important that it be done right.

> *"If a man is to be called a street sweeper, he should*
> *sweep streets even as Michelangelo painted or*
> *Beethoven composed music or Shakespeare wrote poetry.*
> *He should sweep so well that all the hosts in Heaven*
> *and Earth will pause to say, 'Here lived the great*
> *street sweeper who did his job well.'"*

> *Dr. Martin Luther King*

My personal belief has been that there are no bad jobs and no bad workers, only bad matches between the two. Yes, robbing banks is bad, and being a bank robber is bad, but in the realm of honest employment, I do believe that the key to a "good job" and a "good worker" is simply matching the workers' talents and interests properly with the requirements and conditions of the jobs at hand. Couple that match with some decent leadership, and bingo, great things happen.

With the right job match and leadership mix, consistent performance at levels exceeding management expectations is a given.

With those thoughts in mind I can say that the Canadian customs agents who were working on my entry and rifle registration clearly did not represent a good employment match. A customs agent is an important job, a very good one and certainly an occupation of significance. It takes skill to manage the traffic through a border sight, as it requires agents to be able to enforce the laws regarding entry, visas, passports, and identity checks, as well as guarding against the smuggling of contraband material. I am also sure (but less so) that each agent I watched repeatedly fumble through my documentation had some very good work skill existing within. I must say that on this day, I was convinced that the job skills these agents possessed did not support work as a customs agent. The entire time I was held up in this customs office I did not see anyone working there who displayed a shred of enthusiasm for the work they were doing. I am sure that the pay and benefits for these government jobs were good, and in this situation, it might be the remuneration package that provided the bond holding these people to jobs that, to me, they apparently did not enjoy or wish to do.

Within our general population there are also a number of people who are true workaholics and genuinely live to work. Wherever they are, they work with strength and determination regardless of the vocational or environmental circumstances. As an HR person, I always tried to locate and hire these people. Certainly anyone reading this book that was hired by me will agree!

Here's an interesting example of work ethic that has been with me since I first read Aleksandr Solzhenitsyen's great book, <u>A Day in the Life of Ivan Denisovich</u>. In this book Solzhenitsyn describes work in the Russian Gulag prison system that existed under Stalin, and it was truly barbaric. There was no pay (Stalin insisted that political prisoners receive no remuneration), there were no benefits, food rations were miniscule, and living conditions in Siberian prison camps were totally sub-human and deplorable at best. Despite this, prisoner Shukhov, who was assigned to work as a bricklayer, was sent out on work crews in freezing temperatures with rags for clothing, and yet performed his work thoroughly as though he was privately employed and paid wages at the skilled trade level.

At the end of each work day if a worker was late for the work crew's formation to return to the Gulag, that late worker would be severely punished. Shukhov, though, even risked this punishment just to stay at the work site as long as possible to ensure that the brick work he completed that day was straight and level.

Now that's the kind of worker you want to have in your company. Workers like this do exist, and they exist in the suburbs, they exist in the country, and yes, you can also find them in urban America.

Drive Through Canada

The physical drive through Canada to the start of the Alcan highway was a pleasure as the roads were well maintained, the plains area was very open, yet scenic, and there is only a fraction of truck traffic that you see in the U.S.

On this journey I saw first-hand how dependent the U.S. had become on trucks for the delivery of consumer goods. Many stretches of U.S. highway were lined with trucks, literally bumper-to-bumper like unending freight trains extending miles in each direction. These unending freight trains can also be very dangerous behemoths to be near if you are driving a small car.

On that drive through Canada I crossed two unique navigational points of interest. One was when the indicated mileage remaining on my GPS and the trip miles accumulated on my car's odometer were equal and the second was reaching the point I'll call North/North. North/North was the one longitudinal line in North America where magnetic north and true north were the same. It is the only place where your magnetic compass will truly point to the North Pole (earth's rotational axis point). Magnetic north currently rests just west of Ellesmere Island in Northern Canada, which is physically south of the geographic North Pole. Therefore, in North America there is only one true North/North longitudinal line and that is the direct line that starts at the geographical north and travels directly through magnetic north near Ellesmere Island. For accurate navigation calculations, everything east or west of that line requires a deviation allowance to achieve location or destination accuracy. That bit of science may only interest sailors and pilots, however it is interesting to know that magnetic north is slowly drifting toward Siberia, and the very slow advance (millions of years) will someday have a dramatic impact on planet earth by influencing or being influenced by plate tectonics.

Crossing Saskatchewan and Alberta was an easy but long drive, and at the end of that drive was Dawson Creek, British Columbia which is "mile-zero" of the famous Alcan Highway. I had to stop in Dawson Creek and take a photo of the mile-zero road marker as this represented a significant milestone on this new journey.

Dawson Creek was where the most important part of my driving journey began. My travel up to then had been on roads and highways, but that was all they were, just roads and highways. The Alcan highway, a living legend, began as I drove north from Dawson Creek.

CHAPTER 6

THE ALCAN HIGHWAY
(SHORT HISTORY –
INCREDIBLE WORKER ACHIEVEMENTS)

The Alcan Highway represented a significant component of my journey and I had to take time to reflect on it's history. This road was a monumental 1568 mile-long engineering project that by most standards was simply impossible to envision. Construction of that highway required crossing some of the most demanding geography in North America: mountains, rivers, tundra, swamps, and unstable permafrost. Thoughts of constructing this highway to the north dated back to at least the Klondike Gold Rush days of 1896, however any plans made were little more than dreams or wishful thinking as the road north really never materialized. The project was deemed too expensive, an impossible physical endeavor, and therefore abandoned.

THE MILITARY AND WORLD WAR II

*"There never was a good war,
or a bad peace."*

Benjamin Franklin

The engine that pushed construction of the Alcan Highway was World War II (WWII). As a nation, the United States recognized that its strategic Alaska Territory stood without any military defense. The nation also recognized that it needed a route north to assist Russia in the war it was losing to Germany. We wanted to send Russia military supplies. Shipping supply convoys through the North Sea to Russian ports was unacceptable because those convoys were suffering staggering losses. A cargo shipping route over the Pacific Ocean and around Japan to Vladivostock, Russa, would have been suicidal. A supply route through Canada into the Alaskan Territory to eventually reach Russia by air through Siberia would be the only other possible alternative.

Planners knew that building the Alcan Highway would be expensive, the cost in dollars perceived as beyond reach, and the cost in human lives and suffering immeasurable. But think for just a moment about how WWII was going at the time this project was initially planned in 1940. The Japanese Military literally owned the Pacific Ocean and most of the land it touched. The Germans had already conquered and controlled most of Europe, and the German "Blitzkrieg" Juggernaut was proceeding to conquer everything that stood in its path. The military machines of Germany and Japan were on the move, expanding their dictatorial empires, and both were proving to be unstoppable.

Russia was in very desperate times, as the Germans would soon launch an attack through Poland that would literally drive Russia out of their major cities at a cost of millions of human lives. Add to that, Russia's eastern boundaries were anything but secure with Japan once again on the move. Russians never fully recovered from their resounding defeat at the hands of the Japanese in 1905. In military maneuvers, during the Russo-Japanese War, the Japanese completely crushed the Russian Army, and in primarily two naval engagements, Admiral Heihachiro Togo sent the entire Russian Navy (then one of the largest in the world) to the bottom of the sea.

The Russian war machine had been destroyed by the Japanese in 1905 and was about to be ripped apart again by Germany.

To be exact, things were not going very well for anyone standing in the way of Germany or Japan in 1940, and it was clear to most that U.S. involvement in this conflict was a certainty. The turning points for WWII in favor of Allied Forces remained years away and formal participation by the United States did not happen until December of 1941 when Japan attacked Pearl Harbor. In the Pacific theater of war, the U.S. Naval victory at the battle of Midway Island did not take place until June of 1942, the courageous U.S. Marine victory at Guadalcanal did not happen until August of 1942, victory in the Marianas Islands didn't happen until June of 1944, and Iwo Jima Island was not taken until March 1945.

In the European Theater of operations, the "D" Day Invasion at Normandy, France, would not be launched until June of 1942, the fortress at Metz, France, was not secured until November of 1944, and the Battle of the Bulge in Belgium, which represented the final major Nazi military defeat on its western front - was not over until December of 1944.

On the Russian side, the counter offensive attacks against Germany would not take place until late 1942 (with supply help in the form of airplanes, and ordinance supplied through the Alaskan Territory). Stalingrad would not be retaken until early 1943, and would then serve as the trigger for a Russian advance into Germany.

A reliable military supply route to aid Russia was critical, as was as a lifeline supply route to the Alaskan Territory. Then in June of 1942, the Japanese invaded Attu and Kiska Islands in the Aleutians, which only added to the road-building emergency.

The Alcan in 1942 was a much different highway

Construction of the Alcan Highway had reached a critical stage. Building this major roadway was officially underway on March 8, 1942 with construction armies working from the north and the south. This monumental undertaking would be completed in the amazing time of just over eight months on October 25, 1942.

Today and since the end of the war, the Alcan Highway has drawn adventurous people from around the world. On my travel up the Alcan, I met people from all over the U.S. (Florida to California) and even crossed paths with a group of motorcyclists from the Czech Republic (I traveling north and they south). These seasoned bikers stayed at a hotel adjacent to mine in Watson Lake, BC, and were riding a collection of motorcycles of all descriptions (Harleys, Yamahas, Hondas, BMWs) on an expedition from the Artic Circle to San Francisco.

The local folks did not take much notice of the "biker gang" and told me that groups like these rode through town all the time. The locals also advised me that the motorcycle volume through town had increased appreciably, which they attributed to the increased gasoline prices. Fuel at the gas stations in town was running over thirty percent higher than I had paid in the US (liters converted to U.S. gallons). That price difference would serve as a significant deterrent. This collection of motorcycles was interesting to me, and seeing Czech license plates on motorcycles traveling the Alcan struck me as unusual or somewhat out of place.

Motorcycles of all types with this decal on each bike

The physical driving challenges however were not what they once were, as road improvements on the Alcan had been dramatic. My trip north on the Alcan took six days only because I elected to make time to stop along the way to visit and explore. In contrast, my return south on the Alcan was more direct, as I crossed the entire highway in just two days. For the most part it was simply "set the cruise control and sit back and relax."

CHAPTER 7

NORTH TO WHITEHORSE, YUKON TERRITORY
(THOUGHTS ON EMPLOYEE COMMUNICATIONS AND INVOLVEMENT)

STARS AND BEARS

I had been driving the Alcan all day and began to feel exhausted at around five o'clock. I decided to stop driving at a place called Fort Nelson in British Columbia, get a room, and rest for a day or two. Interesting to find hotel accommodations in this part of the world were pretty Spartan. Regardless, the room rates generally had no discounts as the hotels filled up fast toward evening. The heating-ventilation-air-conditioning (HVAC) systems were pretty basic as well. There was some form of heat for the cold nights and an electric fan for hot nights. Each room had its own "central air."

I reached Ft Nelson and a point that represents the three-hundred mile mark of the Alcan Highway. I couldn't fully imagine the pain and suffering that took place when this road was under construction as each mile extracted a heavy toll on men and machines. The soft soil in the warm weather brought things to a temporary halt, as did the frigid cold, but the work continued without rest. I felt a tinge of guilt knowing that I was cruising along the Alcan, very comfortably at a speed of sixty miles an hour, when the army of men building this road, working from the north and the south, were lucky to make six miles a day, working hard seven days a week for eight and a half months. The builders of this highway were very special people, and to quote Tom Brokaw, they were members of "The Greatest Generation."

Before turning in for the night, I stopped at a store in town for some supplies and struck up a conversation with a few of the locals who appeared to be just milling about the place. This store sold a variety of general merchandise items and also offered a good selection of coffee products. The coffee made this store a gathering place for some of the local town people. Now, there wasn't much to see in Ft. Nelson, but these folks were enthusiastically telling me about all the special sites in town. They were certainly very proud of their town and most of the comments were positive and reflected their pride. (Sort of like people talking about their jobs when they're away from work.)

One individual did gripe about some problems in the area that needed to be addressed, "this ain't right, and that ain't right, and this is a big problem, etc." He seemed to be one of those individuals who simply found it hard to be positive and focused too much on problems, complaints, and name calling.

Interestingly, I'd never found chronically complaining people to be very helpful at work when it came to problem resolution. They were always so negative and made every problem worse with their name calling and unflattering labeling of others (ethnic groups primarily) as lazy, stupid, or worthless.

Complainers are always part of the problem and rarely part of the resolution. It's best to do what you can to avoid these types unless you happen to be a therapist with a ton of free time on your hands.

Name calling rarely elicits any good results unless it is positive name calling. In a situation where you believe someone is ungrateful and you tell them they are an ingrate, you've solved nothing. Avoid name calling, and where possible, avoid those who resort to name calling to justify their position or advance their interests. For that reason I personally avoid Washington DC.

People like to hear positive things about themselves, true or not. Let me give you an example of a study on labeling people that I have always loved. This is a true study that falls into the category of "lessons to be learned and applied." It was reported in "Personnel Psychology, Inc" by Ross Stagner a few years ago. The title of the article was "The gullibility of personnel managers" and in it researchers reported that they tested a group of personnel managers who were attending a professional conference. The researchers explained to this large group that they wanted them to take a very confidential personality profile test, and once the test was completed they would be asked to provide their evaluation regarding the accuracy of the test results. It was stressed that the matter would be handled in total confidentiality and asked that each respondent answer the test questions truthfully and to the best of his or her knowledge. It was one of those personality profile, true/false, multiple choice tests where there were no right or wrong answers.

Tests were completed, and the next day the researchers returned with the results for each person. Again they stressed the confidentiality of the test and gave each participant his or her test results. There was a catch. The researchers wanted to measure this test's validity and reliability. What the test respondents did not know was that the test providers had prepared two sets of feedback reports for the group. The first test results handed out were made up and fake. More important than that, each person got the same identical report, worded precisely the same and those reports were stuffed with phony-baloney crap like the horoscope stuff you read on the table mats of a Chinese restaurant. Also the feedback report was mostly positive or flattering with comments like: "You pride yourself as an independent thinker ...", "You have a great deal of unused capacity which you have not turned to your advantage", "You prefer a certain amount of change and variety and become dissatisfied when hemmed in by restrictions and limitations." And the topper: "At times you are extroverted, affable, sociable, while at other times you are introverted, wary, reserved." (What, pray tell, does that mean?)

Now, when these personnel managers were asked to evaluate how accurate this report described them, fifty percent marked the description as "amazingly accurate," forty percent marked the description as "rather good," and ten percent rated the description as about half and half. Incredible but true, ninety percent of the respondents said, "Yeah, that's me." People, certainly HR/Personnel Managers, like to frame themselves in a positive light.

When the researchers tried to hand out the true evaluations to the group for evaluation, it was a disaster. People in the group knew that they had been had, and the science from this scientific study was over.

In my HR career I often thought about that study when I heard a manager start to draw generalizations about individuals or groups of people, maybe yes and maybe no, almost always no.

BIG PROBLEMS

People problems are not big problems, and they can always be resolved.

While in Ft Nelson I had an opportunity to look at some things that were really big, and experience a problem that had the potential to be a very big personal problem.

Toward evening I drove to a place outside of town to take in and enjoy the sun setting over the beautiful Canadian Rockies. The sky was crystal clear and it looked to be a great night to spend some time staring at the stars to identify or pick out a few of the constellations. This was where I got to thinking about the truly BIG picture of life on earth as I stared at what Carl Sagan called the "billions and billions of stars." Now, I will admit that I'm no Carl Sagan and have certainly had many problems trying to identify planets or find constellations, but taking time to look at and think about the stars sent my mind off contemplating the really big things that were out there. I decided that some of those constellations had to have been named or "invented" by early man experimenting with drugs. Pray tell how could you contrive a horse in the heavens based on four stars? That took some very creative imagination. I could identify a few constellations, and as you might suspect, Orion was certainly one of those.

I took out my handy dandy "Smithsonian star finder planisphere" that I brought with me from home. This ingenious device had the appearance of a large circular slide rule with all the stars and constellations clearly laid out on the center of the wheel and all I need to do was dial in the month, day, and time on the outer dial to view a diagram of the sky overhead identified east to west, north to south. In the dimming light I dialed in the current month, day, and time for a view of the heavens, and right before my eyes on the planisphere was a chart of the heavens with all the constellations identified as well as their location overhead. Unfortunate for me, standing this far north in August I would have to wait until three in the morning to see Orion. Maybe with a very early start in the morning, Orion would still be visible in the sky.

For thousands of years people have been doing exactly what I was doing that evening. At every corner of the earth people stare into the sky with wonder, contemplating the size, distance, and enormity of the stars and the heavens. The night sky is truly a captivating and marvelous sight.

Viewing the stars can bring new meaning to the word big as compared to people issues. When I think big here are some of the things that come to mind that may serve as a reality check. First, if you add up the mass of our sun (our star) and all the planets in our solar system, including the giants Jupiter and Saturn, the sun will still represent 99.85 percent of the total mass. That is big and the sun is still growing. Eventually, before our sun evolves into a white dwarf, it will continue to grow and ultimately consume the earth and all earth-like planets. Granted, this will take time (several million years), but when that happens, there will be some significant global warming taking place as 10,000 degrees Fahrenheit would melt a lot of icebergs.

Now if you want more of what is big, think about this: If you replaced our star with the super giant Betelgeuse from the constellation Orion, that star is so big (eight-hundred times larger than our sun) it has a circumference that would extend beyond the orbit of Mars! To put big into a distance perspective, consider this: In 2005 the United States launched a rocket to Pluto for exploration, and that rocket will be traveling at speeds of 36,000 miles per hour, and it will take nearly ten years to arrive at its destination. Those big numbers bewilder me 36,000 miles per hour for 87,600 hours!

Big things are out there to contemplate on any clear evening staring at the stars. The colossal size of the universe and distances between the stars served as a constant reminder that our human problems are comparatively so very small and human problems can always be resolved.

On this night the sky was fascinating. A fresh breeze was blowing big puffy clouds through space, stars were visible between those clouds and the silence of it all held me spellbound. Finding stars and constellations had always been a difficult activity for me. My star finder made this hunt much easier, and I am confident that I located a few prominent ones maybe even fair-guessed at a few more. This star finding activity had me so consumed in thought and busy trying to locate constellations that I unintentionally wandered a little too far down the trail and away from my car.

Suddenly, there was a loud rustling noise in the bushes directly in front of me, and I was instantly paralyzed. What the hell could it be, and why did I wander this far from my car without a decent light. Damn, I had no knife, no gun, and my pepper spray was buried so deep in my luggage that it might never be found. If it was a bear, what should I do? Maybe shove this, now useless, plastic star finder down his throat?

The noise in the bushes continued and my heart started beating at a supersonic pace. I thought about all the articles I'd read regarding bears and what to do when you encounter one, but my paralysis seemed to have captured my brain as well. I managed to shout in a voice that I hoped would be tough sounding, but I know didn't mask over the nervousness and fear that held me frozen in place. I continued to talk loud and then threw a large stone in the general direction of the noise. The noise in front stopped, but why? Was it a bear, and was he now trying to circle me to size up his next meal? Was my imagination running out of control? My paralysis eased up and I started to back away slowly and continued making "threatening" noises. In the movies this seemed to be where the dumb bastard trying to get away managed to fall over a rock or tree branch, but somehow I managed to stay on both feet and continued to back away.

The one thing I was most thankful for was that I did not lock the car doors and wouldn't be fumbling with a key. Eventually, I felt that I was close enough to my car to make a run for it and did just that. I hastily jumped into the front seat and in a fraction of a second had the doors locked (like a bear would bother to use the door latch) then turned on the headlights and honked the horn. I did not see a thing on the trail behind me, and yet my heart was still pounding as I nervously started the car, put it into drive, then made my way back into town. My astronomical research was over for this night; star finding would have to wait for another clear sky at a new bear-free location.

When we are operating outside our comfortable and safe daily human environment, conditions can change from hunter to hunted at an accelerated pace.

Interestingly, this very same type of encounter happened again later in my travel. When it took place, I was more emboldened as I had a loaded rifle on my lap. Though a Smithsonian Star Finder was a unique and interesting device, when it came to bear encounters in the boreal forest, I tended to favor a loaded rifle.

The Park Service in Alaska and ADF&G will tell you that it is important to wear a bell attached to your clothing to sound a ring notifying bears that you are getting near, so you don't surprise them as you approach (it's not a good idea to surprise bears). My fear was that the bell would only serve as a dinner bell allowing a bear to track its next meal (me). Here too, my preference: a loaded rifle over a dinky bell.

There was a hunter in Canada a few years ago who was killed and partially eaten by a bear before the hunter's companions, belatedly, came to his rescue. Ironically, it was a bear that this hunter was hunting, and the bear managed to easily conceal his location, double back, turned the tables if you will, and then stalked the hunter. It was a rapid shift from the hunter to the hunted.

I would admit to a fear of large predators and had no problem surrendering this area of the woods to any bear that might want it. Once I pledged to surrender all the oceans to sharks after an encounter I had fishing near Daytona Beach, Florida. It happened when I was surf fishing with my oldest son, Will, who was only ten or eleven years old at the time. It was a beautiful day with very little wind blowing, and the bait fish were running near shore. My son wanted to catch a shark, so I told him to cast his bait near where the bait fish were jumping as something big had to be chasing them, and it might be a small shark. He had no luck and eventually gave up, so I decided to try to catch one for him (be a guide, you see).

I began chasing after the different schools of bait fish without success and eventually became so focused on the jumping schools of bait fish that I allowed myself to get drawn into deeper water, so deep that I had to hold the fishing rod over my head to cast as the water was near neck high. Then I realized I was fishing out beyond the sand bar and actually casting back toward the shore when something large swam right between my legs. It is not possible for me to describe the instant fear that shot through my body. I scrambled to shore as fast as I could move and I am 100 percent positive that any shark in the entire Daytona Beach area was fully aware of my panicked condition. I did not see what type of fish it was, but I can tell you that my fear went beyond imagination as that fish was large enough to hit the inside of both of my spread out legs as it passed beneath me. I thought I too may have shifted from the hunter to the hunted. I've never done that again, in fact while I still fish the ocean surf, I never venture out into water that is even knee deep, basically surrendering the sea and seventy percent of the earth's surface to any shark that wants it.

Two years ago I took my two sons on a fishing charter in Florida, and we were fishing in the Gulf Stream just four miles off the coast near Palm Beach. The Gulf Stream water was ever so clear on this hot day and very inviting. We were having a great time fishing, and

I was watching my youngest son, Eric, trying to land a fish that was giving him a tough time, as this fish probably weighed in the twenty to twenty-five pound range. At the same time, I was thinking how nice it would be to just jump into the beautiful water for a nice refreshing swim. Eric was finally able to pull his fish up to the side of our boat, and just as we reached down with the landing net to retrieve it, a large bull shark shot out of the deep and literally ate half of the fish in one bite right before our eyes. It happened so fast it was like a cannon ball shot out of the dark.

Call me chicken, but sharks are apex predators and are free to swim the ocean with no fear of running into me.

Before leaving Ft. Nelson I did two things. First I walked to the local ice arena to watch a group of young kids going through their power drills in preparation for the pending hockey season. These little kids were fantastic. Tiny little bodies zooming around the ice arena wearing oversized helmets. Watching them in action was just great fun.

Second, encouraged by some local town people, I drove out to the Ft. Nelson airport to see the world's biggest commercial helicopter. I was told by local residents about this helicopter with such enthusiasm that I had to make some time to see this flying machine even though one resident advised that I would not be able to talk to the helicopter crew because they only spoke a foreign language; she said it was German. Knowing the origin of this machine, I asked if the language might be Russian and not German. To this she said she didn't know, but it was probably one of those!

The helicopter was a Russian-made machine being used by the Canadian oil companies to carry oil rigs and large oil rig parts out to the various work sites as there were no roads leading to the drilling rigs. Now this helicopter was a giant, and a Blackhawk helicopter might just be able to fly inside this monster. You really had to stand next to this beastly giant to feel its unequalled enormity. Flying this helicopter required a ten man crew and its massive turbine engines burned an incredible one liter of fuel per second (even oil companies used this monster sparingly). It was no Betelgeuse, but as helicopters go it had to be the king and was an impressive sight.

ASKING QUESTIONS

The airport visit proved to be a good learning experience for me. The airport only had a few fixed-wing bush planes, but did hanger numerous helicopters of various makes. The helicopters were used to transport workers to the various oil drilling sites and to transport surveyors and other oil company workers.

What I found interesting was the amount of information that I was given about the airport, the history of the various flight services, flight conditions in the area, and background on the equipment being employed. I simply showed some interest, asked questions and they showered me with answers.

Asking good questions is the key to securing business information and/or conducting competent interviews (hunting, if you will). I'm one of those individuals who will ask a lot of questions. This practice has become ingrained in my brain, and at times it seems to be automatic, in part, because of the "conditioning" I put myself through in years of disciplined employment interviewing, and in part because it's just the way I operate as an individual. Asking questions (and listening) is the most fantastic way I know to acquire knowledge and discover truths. It is absolutely amazing to me what people will tell you if you simply ask a question and show even slight interest in the answer provided . . . absolutely amazing!

I sometimes find myself in situations where I ask questions when I fully know the answer and may even know the answer better than the person being questioned (I think it's called playing dumb). Here you want to know if the respondent not only knows anything about the subject, but how honest they are, how they came by this knowledge, and how willing they are to share their knowledge. People, in general, are willing to give enormous amounts of information and show you that they have knowledge particularly if it involves the work they do: "You see, I am important. I am somebody ... this is my job, here is what I do."

Business leaders, like all hunters, need to be inquisitive, collecting information and then putting that information to use constructively in their organization.

A few years ago I had the privilege to take part in a special management tour of the Toyota manufacturing plant in Kentucky. This was a very interesting manufacturing operation for a couple reasons; first, it was the plant that made the car that I drove on this journey north (I must add that they did an excellent job as well) and more importantly it was one of those successful U.S. located automobile manufacturing plants that continued to grow and expand. Instead of layoffs and closures they had grown to nearly ten-thousand workers (probably more as of this writing). The expanding workforce was unique as others in the car industry (I need not mention) seemed to be doing the just opposite, and yet the pay and benefits for workers at Toyota was relatively the same as any U.S. automobile manufacturer. At the conclusion of the tour we (the management folks on tour) were allowed to select three workers at random to ask about their Toyota experiences. Now all three that we selected were more than a little apprehensive at first with a large group of suit-and-tie business folks firing questions at them like they were in a corporate board room, but the workers did an excellent job and impressed me with their knowledge of the manufacturing process. These three were all shop floor employees (team members), and what interested me most was at the end of the session I asked them all what was it about Toyota that made it different from other places where they worked. The answer was unanimous and immediate from all three: "Management listens to us. They take time to meet with us and honestly pay attention to what we have to say."

Interesting. Management asks questions and listens.

Keep in mind that managers need to do more than just ask and listen, managers need to take appropriate action based on what they discover. Action taken must correspond to the best interests of the organization's future, and when it comes to manufacturing, those actions must preserve the ability to make products of acceptable cost and quality for the customers.

On a separate management tour of the, then new, General Motors (GM) Saturn plant in Tennessee, I witnessed a monumental effort on the part of GM to listen to workers, albeit through a third party. This was a tour set up to show outside management people what a successful operation they had at Saturn and an attempt, at least on the part of the

United Auto Workers Union (UAW), to sell the Saturn union relations concept to other companies.

The labor relations arena at this Saturn Plant was unique as the labor agreement (some incorrectly referred to these third party agreements as contracts) was not actually a labor agreement as compared to those historically negotiated in normal auto industry practice. GM and the UAW initially agreed on an open, unstructured agreement between the parties, innovative in such a way that it represented a truly unique and courageous approach taken by both management and union. No doubt about it, this was a major effort by GM to try something new and to do it on a grand scale.

The folks who provided the tour (surprisingly all represented employees) were not successful selling anything to me, as I found them less than cooperative when I asked questions regarding manufacturing issues, staffing and assembly schedules. Conversely, Toyota was very open about answering those same questions. Now when I didn't get answers to my questions, I automatically believed that those answers, if provided, would not be favorable to the sales pitch being tossed my way (maybe yes, maybe no). Also, as an old HR person, I saw some plant employment costs on this visit that I thought were excessive, so much so that I would only describe those costs as ones you wanted your competition to be burdened with.

As a general rule in business you must understand that a labor cost problem is not always the amount of pay provided for work being done, it is the amount of pay provided for work not being done. At the Saturn plant I had concerns about work not being done and departed that location a little disappointed. I truly hope this plant is successful for GM as they have clearly invested a monumental amount of capital and energy into it.

Management has to listen and then take appropriate action; it isn't all that easy.

WHO KNOWS WHAT'S REALLY GOING ON?

That brings to mind another interesting question that plagued me often in business and that is: Who knows a job best, and who knows the most about what is going on at a work location? As a past vice president, director, manager and supervisor I can assure you that is isn't always management.

Let me relate a work story. My father worked as a machinist and tool & die maker coming from what I will call the old school. He worked hard to develop his skills in the trade and took great pride in his work and individualism. He always viewed the skilled trade department of a manufacturing operation as something very special. Working there clearly required special talent and training.

Toward the end of his working career, my father's employer was engaged in activities needed to make the operation more efficient and cost conscious. The company hired a team of talented engineers to time study every operation (including the machine shop) and set work time standards for the completion of all jobs going through the plant. The engineers came to him with a new set of time standards for each job. Never did they ask for his input or listen to anything he suggested, nor did the management of the company show any interest in worker ideas. When he offered advice, they politely dismissed his input and proceeded on their predetermined course, which was basically telling him how much time anyone in the skilled trades area could spend doing each job going through the machine shop. As example, part number X5555 would need two hours on the lathe, then one hour on the milling machine before going to the surface grinder for thirty minutes of finish work. That was fine and dandy, and my father understood (but didn't like) the need to standardize the process. What frustrated my father was that he was doing the work, but they would not listen to the ideas he had regarding making the machine shop operation more productive and cost-efficient.

Now I can tell you, without qualification, that the person who knows the job best is the person doing it every day. My father wanted the company to arrange the work flow differently. In the X5555 example, it would take three and a half hours to get that part through the machine shop, and my father's frustration was that the company didn't allow him to rearrange the work flow. He knew how to set up the lathe, milling machine, and surface grinder to operate simultaneously, which would have cut the time on X5555 from three and a half hours to less than two hours. This company wouldn't listen to any suggestions from the shop floor. My father became more frustrated with the changes taking place and lack of management interest and decided that it was time for him to take early retirement. The company later went out of business in part, I believe, because they missed out on opportunities to listen to the people who knew best how to do their jobs.

Here's another real world example of not listening that exists today at a place I will call Company X (pseudonym, of course). Company X closely measures all their manufacturing steps and has a unique incentive structure to keep people working fast and hard. They pay a fair hourly wage to plant employees and then add an incentive pay, based on production. This incentive bonus can be very large and may equal or exceed the worker's gross pay for the year. The incentive is paid once a year and is the engine that drives Company X's manufacturing. On a tour of Company X with other business managers a few years ago, the HR Director for Company X advised tour participants that his company did not care about happy workers all they wanted were productive workers. Hey, you figure. I know if I am unhappy I want to share that unhappiness with the person or organization making me feel that way.

I met an industrial psychologist once (a Dr. Frank Ezzo, PhD) who was fond of saying that "Misery does not like company. Misery only likes miserable company." Dr. Ezzo made a very good point!

On our guided tour of the manufacturing plant I also saw a lot of unhappy faces. Our Company X tour guide explained that they were committed to measuring all work being done throughout the operation, including the machine shop and skilled trade areas. As our tour group walked through the machine shop, I noticed a machinist standing next to and operating an old machine called a shaper. I also noticed that there were at least four milling machines in the immediate area that were sitting idle. Now, if you have even basic knowledge of machine shop tools you know that any job that can be done on an old shaper can be done faster and better on a milling machine.

Curiosity got the best of me, and I had to drift away from the guided tour to talk to this machinist at the shaper. First, I commented on the machine and its age. The machinist replied that it was a good old machine and jokingly added that most of the shapers around today were in museums. I saw that he was cutting a key-way on a shaft and asked him why he wasn't using one of the milling machines for this job. He just gave me a big smile and said; "The best rate is on this machine."

He knew that the shaper machine time rate was wrong (stupid), and he recognized that I knew it was wrong, but using the shaper for this job was easy and under the management measuring system it provided better pay. It was not the best, most efficient use of time and labor, but it did provide better personal pay. Company X management obviously did not do a good job of securing this worker's input on the work process or involve him in work flow design. The company just gave him the rates and told him how to do it. Trust me, when you tell people how to do a job they generally do just that (maybe) and no more.

"Never tell people how to do things.
Tell them what to do and they will
Surprise you with their ingenuity."

General George S. Patton

Several years ago I happened to be working with a consultant on some employee involvement training issues with my company, and he shared with me an account that dramatically demonstrates who knows the job best.

This account took place at a manufacturing plant in a midwest city where the parts being made were relatively heavy and had to be placed into metal containers approximately four feet square and three feet deep to be transported by forklift truck between finishing operations. The assembly process was very straight forward, and when a machine operator filled the metal transportation container near the work station, he simply turned on a light over the machine as a signal to a forklift driver to stop and remove the full container and drop off an empty one.

What happened, too often, was that a machine operator would turn on the light requesting a forklift operator, but the forklift was tied up at other work stations, and the machine operator simply had to wait. Remember, this is a problem because it represents pay for work not being done as the worker is, involuntarily, standing idle. Production stops waiting for that forklift.

The manufacturing manager was called on by supervisors to buy additional forklifts to remedy the delays, however the manager was reluctant because the forklift machines were very expensive, and he thought they already had an adequate number of those machines.

This manager went to the workers for help. In essence he wanted the forklift operators and machine operators (those who knew the jobs best) to work on a solution. He set them up as a team and arranged some training for problem solving after which the workers launched their examination of the forklift problem, or more correctly stated, production delay problem. Once engaged in this problem solving process, workers recognized that adding an additional forklift was not the problem, it was only a possible solution.

The workers recommended some changes in how the finishing machines were set up and an expansion of the marshalling area used for empty containers. In addition, they asked that the four-by-four containers be placed on wheels or some type of dolly that would allow the operator to push the full container out of the way and then push an empty four-by-four container into its place.

The recommendations were implemented by the manager, and not only did they remedy the delay in manufacturing (pay for work not being done evaporated) but with the worker-recommended changes they found out that they had too many forklift trucks already and eliminated the expense of buying a new forklift machine. Of course, an added plus was that the workers fully accepted and bought into these production changes because they had recommended them. The changes made in this manufacturing process were not dictated to the workers, the changes were their own, involved workers now had ownership. Real work motivation, you see, comes from within and it is all voluntary.

Who knows what work is really going on? Managers need to make time to ask and listen to the person doing that job day in and day out. It would also pay to reexamine the historic study done at the Hawthorne Plant of Western Electric Co. in the 1930's. This study supposedly analyzed work performance changes resulting from lighting level adjustments. It ended up proving that listening to workers made the difference in performance, not lighting changes. Workers were asked for their input and responded positively. The Hawthorne study has been part of or referenced in every management text book since the 1930's --- nothing new --- managements poor memory will always keep training consultants busy.

I must also note that at the Ft. Nelson, BC, airport I met with and talked to many people; managers, pilots, owners and airport staff. The person I learned the most from was a young man whose job was washing airplanes and helicopters. He didn't stand on the top rung of the business ladder for sure, but he did know an enormous amount about the airport's operation, the flying machines on the field, and other things like what flying machines were best maintained, which ones to avoid, who were the best pilots, and the cost of flight operations out of that airport. He knew what was going on.

Bison had an attitude

FORT NELSON TO WATSON LAKE

I found myself back on track and running north once again, and what a wonderful run it turned out to be. The drive through the Canadian Rockies was spectacular. Places like Stone Mountain, Summit Lake

Pass, Muncho Lake, Steamboat Creek, the Sentinel Range, and the Barricade Range were awesome sites to see and large game animals were plentiful from start to finish. I could not, however, help but think about the extreme hardships the soldiers and engineers endured building this stretch of the highway - beautiful landscape yes, but this terrain had to be a road construction nightmare.

Twice in route, I had to stop my car to let bison cross the highway, and once I stopped for a long parade of caribou. The second stop for bison was the best as there had to be seventy to eighty bison surrounding my car. These were wild animals, very large, heavy, slow, and cantankerous looking beasts, and they appeared to have no fear regarding the traffic on the highway (although my car was the only one for miles in either direction). Most animals try to give humans and their cars a wide berth but these guys had an attitude and showed it . . . they really impressed me. Further down the road I saw where this lack of vehicle concern carried with it a price as a few bison lay on their side, motionless at the road's edge. The wide array of major vehicle parts scattered about at these accident locations told me that whatever vehicles hit these behemoths also paid a steep price.

Twice I had to surrender the Alcan to bison

This stretch of the Alcan Highway proved to be the most impressive part of my drive from a geological and wild animal standpoint. I saw both whitetail deer and mule deer. Then, later a large heard of those majestic elk and some mountain sheep. I did not see a single moose, and this was prime moose country as well. There was still a long highway ahead of me with more glorious sights that I was sure would include a few moose and maybe a nice big bull.

The drive from Fort Nelson to Watson Lake took about six hours and at the midway point there was a fishing lodge that was something out of a dream book. The Northern Rockies Lodge sat right on the shore of magnificent Munco Lake. This beautiful log cabin resort offered hunting, fishing, site seeing tours, and was a five star location for anyone who wanted to explore the beautiful northern Rocky Mountains or anyone who was looking for an enchanting place to sit, read, and think. The lodge offered tours through this grand country that can be arranged on foot, boat, airplane or helicopter. If you wanted to smell and feel the Northern Rockies this was the place to stay . . . it was marvelous.

The geographic architecture displayed throughout these mountains impressed me much more than the architecture of the Grand Canyon. You could clearly see signs of early mountain formation and the consequent millions of years of erosion. Winding through these mountains, I saw many formations of alluvial fans created by heavy rains, melting snow, washouts, and floods. One mountain called Folded Mountain, in particular, displayed signs of the powerful forces created by the moving tectonic plates that formed the Canadian Rockies. One side of Folded Mountain adjoined a fault in the earth, and when the mountain was pushed up by the crashing plates it revealed layers of earth sediment along the cliff side of the mountain representing the buildup of the floor of a past, long-lost ocean.

My photography skills are not great, and I regret that I was not able to get a good picture of this magnificent mountain, because it was spectacular. Those sedimentary layers representing millions of years of time have to be any geologists dream come true.

My continued drive along the Alcan Highway was rich, bountiful and ever so rewarding.

I stopped the next night at a motel just off the highway. It was an unpretentious looking old building but looked to be clean and reasonably well maintained. There was a large sign in the front that read "Under New Management." Those signs are interesting because we read them and automatically assume that the old management must have been bad. The signs themselves often imply that it is better now or outright announce that claim. The message conveyed is always that you probably got a bad deal out of the incompetent old management, but we are the good new folks, and we'll take care of you. In truth, we all know that just the opposite may be true, but we intuitively assume that new has to be better.

Did you ever stop to wonder what happened to the old management people? In all likelihood they just moved to another area of the same town, bought into an existing business, and then put a sign out front that reads, "Under New Management." It's a phenomenon called the old management - new management syndrome that perpetuates itself. Retail furniture stores seem to be very good at employing that new management message. Did you ever enter a furniture store that had a new management sign out front and see that the new managers appear to be the same people who have always been running the place?

The new owner and resident manager of this motel was a middle-aged Asian fellow. He was very soft-spoken, slow moving, and a man of few words. I told him that I needed a room for two nights and asked if he had a room with a good view of the mountains. To this, he replied with a head nod indicating yes (actually it would have been difficult to have a room at this location without a view of the mountains as they surrounded the entire town). I also explained that I had a lot of reading to do and asked if the room had good lighting, he responded with a nod. I then asked if the room had a desk that I could work from and got yet another nod from the new manager. He then handed me my room key and said, "Room 104," and gave a nod. Later, I returned to the motel office to request a second desk lamp as I needed more light. The new manager gave a nod. He later delivered the lamp to my room, knocked on the door, and when I opened it, he simply handed me a desk lamp and gave me a nod.

I assumed that this new manager couldn't speak or held a very weak grasp of the English language. On my second day at the motel, I happened to meet the chambermaid and asked if the new manager might have limited English language skills. She said, "Oh no, his English is excellent, he just doesn't like to talk."

It made me wonder why this new owner would purchase a business that, in my opinion, required substantial communication skills. But what the hey, I got my room with a desk and two lamps, so I was happy. Interesting too, five weeks later, on my return trip, I stopped at this same motel and this time my request was for a single night. I got a nod. I asked if the new manager remembered me and got a nod. He then handed me a room key and said, "Room 138," and gave a nod. I thanked him, went to my room to unpack, and in less than twenty minutes I heard a knock on the door. When I opened it the new manager was standing there, he handed me a second desk lamp (that I had not requested), nodded, and walked away. People are interesting, they can be fun, and people are most certainly unique.

Day Two in the Yukon

Back on the Alcan and day two in the Yukon, it got a little wet and cold. My prior concern about being over-packed by adding too much cold weather clothing had now disappeared. You could always take off a layer or two of clothing if it got too hot, but it was impossible to add a coat if you didn't have one with you, as there were no department stores in my prospective hunting area. Weather can change fast in the far north, and I was prepared (Thank you Pack 222).

I was sitting in my hotel room the following day, drinking my morning coffee, looking out at the mountains to the north, and I must say that the mountain sights gave me a feeling of tremendous comfort. The mountains were near and so beautiful, and rain or not, the landscape was spectacular. The beauty gave my morning, and my day, a very tranquil start.

From my second story window I could see some men gathered together near the main road. They appeared to be waiting for a ride to work, possibly one of those "day work" arrangements for general labors.

Not much energy is spent when you recruit day workers. They are needed for some labor activity and are generally paid in cash at the end of each day.

In California I had seen migrant day workers standing on the street corners awaiting work, and when a potential employer drove by, they held up some of their fingers to advise what they wanted as an hourly wage, four, five, six fingers or any wage request that they thought might stop the prospective employment vehicle to pick them up for a day's work (day work, you see). Often when the employment vehicle drove by without stopping, I saw their wage request uniformly drop to one.

Day work seemed to operate in the Yukon much the same as anywhere in North America, but I believe that the minimum wage in Canada is considerably higher than any other place on the North American continent. Not enough fingers on both hands for the minimum wage there.

Watching these workers load into the work van and drive off got me thinking about some rules and ideas regarding the people management business. For any of you people business types, (and we all are) please stay tuned, and I'll share my thoughts on the subject of Human Resource Management in chapter fifteen.

> "Work is one of the few things in life that provides an opportunity to challenge our creativity and measure our accomplishments; without work, life can become soulless. The least we can do is approach it with sincerity and enthusiasm"
>
> Business Management Newsletter,
> Author unknown

DRIVE FROM WATSON LAKE

I left town in the nick of time as the electric power to the entire city shut down. The hotel desk clerk advised that power outages happened all the time in Watson Lake and were often a daily occurrence. I wondered what happened to the people in winter who were dependent on electric heat?

This northern section of the highway weaved in and out of British Columbia and the Yukon Territory, providing spectacular geographic views of the northern Rocky Mountains. A magnetic compass has 360 degrees on its compass rose and here you could direct your attention to any degree on the compass and view sites of unbelievable wilderness beauty. The landscape was awesome.

This leg of my journey also provided an opportunity to meet with an interesting guy who owned and operated a business called Red Wolf Computing in Teslin, Yukon Territory. Now Teslin was not a big community by any measure, but I did know of it from reading a Bush Airplane book about a pilot named Frank Barr. Frank flew a route from Alaska through British Columbia and the Yukon Territory back in the pioneer days of bush flying. Frank flew an airplane that was genuinely unique. It was a Fairchild Pilgrim and a tough old bird.

In the early days of aviation Fairchild was a camera company located in New York State (Long Island, I believe), and when they started doing aerial photography, they could not find a suitable airplane for use as an aerial photography platform. To solve this problem, Fairchild started to design and build airplanes, and they made some dandies. The Fairchild 24 (one of my favorites), the Fairchild 52, and Fairchild 72 were simply great early airplanes and worked very well for aerial photography. They also were employed by early bush pilots, and a pilot named Bob Reeves did some impossible flying in a Fairchild 72 out of Valdez, Alaska (off tidal mud flats to be exact).

Fairchild's Pilgrim was used as both a passenger airplane and a freight hauler. It was an awkward, bulky looking, high-wing airplane with the pilot positioned high on the fuselage and directly behind the airplane's big single radial engine. Interestingly, the pilot was not in contact with, nor could he even see, his passengers who sat below him in the center section of the fuselage. It was a strange, bulky-looking, airplane and yet the Fairchild Pilgrim was a real workhorse that Frank consistently flew through the most difficult and unforgiving terrain, fighting adverse weather conditions that were at times unimaginable.

So as I was driving down the Alcan, getting close to Teslin, thinking about Frank Barr and the old Pilgrim, I saw a sign on the side of the road that read "Red Wolf Computing Teslin, YT." I had been having PC difficulty so I thought, *Hey, why not stop and check it out?* I was certainly happy that I did. It was a pleasant and rewarding visit, and on top of everything else, Red Wolf fixed my PC, taught me a couple new things about PC's (another learning experience), and I was back on the road. I will always remember the friendly assistance from Red Wolf Computing, Teslin, Yukon Territory

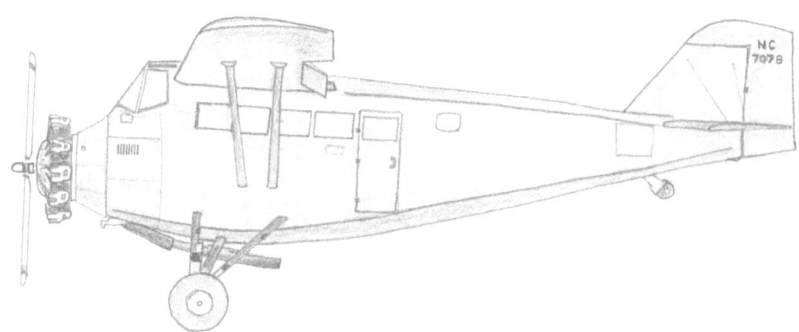

Fairchild Pilgrim

WHITEHORSE YUKON TERRITORY

Whitehorse was a very interesting city with a colorful history going back to the Gold Rush Days. The city also came equipped with a Wal-Mart, two McDonalds, and a Starbucks coffee shop, which had to place it into the big leagues.

Another fascinating historical aspect of Whitehorse was that it was the home of poet Robert W. Service. As an outdoors person I have always loved the poems written by Robert Service: "The Shooting of Dan McGrew," "The Cremation of Sam McGee," and my all time favorite "The Spell of the Yukon." In this part of the world, Robert W. Service rose above the level of legend as his poetry clearly defined the area and its rich history. Service's poems often chronicled the hard times and human pain suffered by the early gold miners of the Klondike Gold Rush. I cannot help but think too that some of his poetic perspective on life's hardships must have been drawn from, or certainly influenced by, the time Robert Service spent driving an ambulance in France during World War I. The death, destruction, and hardship caused by any war can leave mental wounds or unwanted memories that last a lifetime, but the carnage of WWI was particularly gruesome. Working in the field hospitals and transporting the wounded during a war that killed over eight million soldiers had to be very difficult for anyone including Robert Service.

Robert Service had a lighter side and his humor surfaced in his poetry as well. Two of my comical, and clever, favorites were: <u>I Believe</u> and <u>The Ordinary Man</u>. The first may have been written with people managers in mind and the second might apply to the folks back in Normal, Illinois.

Well written poetry is sagacious and serves to generate new ideas, kindling thought "outside the box" in your organization. In chapter sixteen I will reference some training work I did with poet David Whyte. In his training presentation David observes management through a poetic eye in a way that stimulates thought and provokes ideas for business managers at all levels.

My short two-day visit in Whitehorse, Yukon Territory, was fun and an interesting learning experience. I also enjoyed re-reading Robert Service's poems reflecting back to an occurrence years earlier when I climbed a mountain in the Alaska Range, above the tree line, sat on a rock, detached from the rest of the world, to read aloud some of his poetry. Those were rewarding personal moments for me separated from the chaos of work, embracing the quiet surroundings and at peace in nature.

My visit to Whitehorse rated as one of the most memorable components of my travel north and was certainly enjoyable. Whitehorse has a defined character and is a place I planned to visit again someday. But time had arrived to pack my bags and prepare for the final leg of my drive north on the Alcan highway.

One Alcan Highway experience eluded me. It was strange almost unreal to know that I had driven over 3,500 miles, saw more wild large game animals than I could count, passed through excellent moose habitat, and yet I had not seen a single moose, cow or bull! I hoped it wasn't a harbinger of things to come.

CHAPTER 8

GREAT FRIENDS AND THE ALCAN ENDS
(PEOPLE MAKE THE DIFFERENCE)

The final destination on this journey north was Fairbanks, Alaska, and I met up with some very good friends, Girts and Linda Upesleja. Girts, my friend since we served together in the US Army, and his wife Linda are two genuine, sincere, and high quality people.

Throughout life we encounter thousands of people, some of them we like, some of them we do not, and then some we meet are those special ones who we choose to hold as our best friends. It is a choice we make and not a decision that is forced on us. Personal friendships can easily be described as the heart and soul of our life on earth. Friendships are special relationships that give more meaning to what we do everyday by adding laughter, companionship, and support. Without good friends life on earth would have less meaning and certainly be less fun.

For most of us the strongest and most lasting and bonding friendships are those made early in life, generally when we first leave home and strike out on our own. High school students who head off to college establish special friendships with other students they meet from different parts of the USA, different counties, and different walks of life. Many of those initial friendships, despite any future physical distances, last a lifetime.

The Army was my initial departure from home and there I met two friends when I shipped overseas who were of that special variety. Mike Weekly from Northern California and Girts Upesleja who now lives in Fairbanks, Alaska, were my chosen friends and "Army buddies." We served together overseas, helped one another through difficult times, went on military maneuvers together, bivouacked (camped outside) in the winter snow, and had tremendous fun on duty and off. Over the years we have maintained close contact despite the distance in miles from our homes. We three old Army buddies have visited each other in our home states on a number of occasions and will forever love to reminisce about those old Army days and military experiences. Lasting bonds of friendship truly rate at the top of the most wonderful treasures in life, and I genuinely looked forward to seeing Girts and his wife Linda once again in Fairbanks. Oh yes, Fairbanks represented a significant milestone on this trip as well, because it is was the official termination point on the fantastic Alcan Highway!

**Girts & Linda Upesleja in Fairbanks and
Mike Weekly in N. California.**

In Fairbanks, those 1568 miles of Alcan Highway were behind me, and I accomplished that long sought after goal. I also discovered that I made it from start to finish without as much as a scratch on my car. I could forget any of the old horror stories I had heard about the Alcan Highway having dangerous and treacherous road surfaces that were pre-ordained to destroy my car. There was a time in Alcan Highway history where it was an authentic monster of a road to travel and many stories had been related to me that would make me think the highway had not changed much since 1942, but it certainly had changed.

Today the Alcan is a much different road, and its surface is now paved from start to finish absent some short stretches of rebuilding construction. The Alcan Highway is also superbly maintained by the Canadian Department of Highways.

I did not need a four-wheel-drive truck with protective skid plates, protective radiator guards, and headlight covers. Nor did I need to carry multiple spare tires or massive quantities of emergency rations to cross the fabled Alcan. This drive up the Alcan was easy, the sights spectacular, and the journey was great fun from start to finish.

The good news for me was that I arrived ahead of schedule and time was available before my hunt started to take a few more side trips in Alaska. My first plan was to visit Girt's daughter, husband, and new granddaughter in Wasilla, Alaska, and then visit with my nephew, Allan Perunko and his family in Anchorage. The driving distance between Fairbanks, Wasilla, and Anchorage was great, but the weather for this excursion was splendid. Girts and I made this trip together with him pointing out many new and interesting sights along the way. We stopped on the Parks Highway just south of Fairbanks to take a photograph of Mt. McKinley framed in a clear blue sky, in pilot terminology, a CAVU (clear and visibility unlimited) sky. There were no clouds or obstructions, and I photographed the entire mountain without weather restrictions, from a distance of hundreds of miles. The visits we made in Wasilla and Anchorage were pure enjoyment and the time taken on this side trip went by ever so fast. As an added bonus, Girts did all the driving.

The Big One on a CAVU day – 100's of miles distant

My nephew served as staff sergeant and F-15 crew chief in the US Air Force stationed at Elmendorf Air Force Base in Anchorage. On this visit, Alan gave Girts and I a hands-on tour of this impressive air force base. Those F-15's are spectacular fighter aircraft and, while not conceivable, it would have been awesome to just jump into the cockpit and take one for a flight (granted some additional pilot-skills training might be needed). The F-15 might not qualify as a very good bush plane for moose hunting, but it is one of my all time favorite military fighters, and the tour Allan gave us was a wonderful learning experience.

Later on my hunt I saw those same USAF, F-15 fighters flying high overhead in central Alaska. They operated with hunting precision as Orion would in earth's airspace and were truly impressive flying machines.

With my visits in Wasilla and Anchorage over, it was time for me to return to Fairbanks, and time for my long awaited hunt to begin.

Over the Alcan without a scratch

CHAPTER 9

THE HUNT BEGINS
(COMMENTS ON GENDER ROLE CHANGES)

The first leg of my hunt was by air in a bush plane followed by a ride on pack horses to a base camp located in the middle of a very large Alaskan game management area near Fairbanks, Alaska. This particular game management hunting area did not allow the use of any engines for land transportation. Absent the flight in by bush plane there were <u>no engines</u> or motorized vehicles of any kind permitted. For me this restriction established a hunting area that personified The last frontier of the last frontier.

A hunting acquaintance from the Cleveland area was flying into Fairbanks to start a separate hunt for brown bear, and I agreed to pick him up at the airport upon his arrival. Picking him up was no problem for me as I was in Fairbanks at the time and would enjoy his company on the drive to the location where flights for our separate hunts would depart. This acquaintance was a seasoned big game hunter and was the person who put me in touch with the hunting outfitter I used for my hunt. He had hunted with this outfitter on several occasions and gave him an unqualified excellent recommendation as both a hunter and a guide.

We arrived at our motel near the starting point late that night and were up early the next morning and very eager to get started on our hunts. We were both scheduled to fly into our respective hunting base camps at around the same time even though we were going to hunt at locations miles apart. The base camps were used as the key jump-off point for small groups of hunters. From a base camp, hunting excursions of any distance required the use of smaller, more temporary, camp arrangements referred to as a spike camps. Our flights were initially delayed and then cancelled on day one due to high winds and unstable flight conditions. All hunters waiting for departure were visibly disappointed, however the pilot received no argument from me as the winds were ripping through the valley at near hurricane force. In truth, if the pilot decided to fly with conditions so poor, I would have asked for a new pilot.

The two of us decided to make the most of the situation and take a tour of the area traveling off-road as best we could in my four-door Toyota Avalon. The weather conditions were dry, so my Avalon quickly turned into a pseudo back-woods vehicle. If a rainstorm had hit the area we would have been in deep trouble as I, honestly, took the car too far back into the mountains, getting there only by riding the tops of the dry road/trail ruts made by real off-road machines. Luck was with us, and even though I may have pushed the Avalon too far, we still made it back to a hard surface road without getting stuck and with no damage to the car -- an amazing feat given the horrible trail surface conditions.

The landscape/terrain we covered was impressive, the air smelled so fresh and the feel of the woods was on us. Our tour that day was a fun learning experience and a warm-up for the hunt. One thing we learned was that hunting success in this general area had not been good since the season opened. Poor results were being reported by everyone we met. A store retailer advised that her husband and two sons had been out hunting moose all week, from Sun-up to Sun-down, and did not see a single moose. On checking into our motel, I talked with two disgruntled out-of-state hunters who were busy packing their gear for departure to the Anchorage airport and home. Both had been hunting hard all week and between them were only able to locate and shoot a single caribou. One hunter showed us the caribou's antlers which were only of moderate size. The men were two unhappy individuals, and one of them elected not to speak a single word while he put away an expensive rifle into an equally expensive shipping/travel case for his flight home. It was obvious that he did not have an opportunity to use the rifle and was visibly upset. Meeting with other local people yielded the same unpromising feedback. I later surmised that overall hunting success that season had fallen well below expectations, and even professional guides were batting below five hundred.

Two Outstanding Workers

The flight delay on this first day of our hunt allowed me an opportunity to witness two very outstanding people at work achieving exceptional results. I feel compelled to comment on these two individuals as they were truly impressive workers and personify excellence in employment.

The first individual worked at a lodge nearby where we had dinner. The lodge sat at the west side of the main hard surfaced road near our departure point. There was only one employee at the lodge, a pleasant woman named Chris who, from an employment standpoint, covered all the bases at the lodge. This lodge had a horseshoe shaped bar where approximately a dozen patrons sat being waited on (a job on its own). It also had a beer/alcohol carryout counter setup, adjacent to the bar, arranged to accommodate some type of law Alaska has requiring take-out beer and alcohol be sold as a separate business. In addition to tending to the bar patrons, this sole employee took care of all sales at this second counter. The lodge also had two dinning areas with eight to ten tables each, and yes, the one worker at the lodge also took care of taking dinner orders and table cleaning/preparation. The cooking area for the lodge was located along one wall between the dining areas and the bar (actually it was in the hallway) and yes again, this one-person army did all the cooking and meal preparation. It was awesome just watching this woman work, she was a human dynamo, and on top of everything else she maintained a very pleasant disposition. Add to that, our dinners were very good and served timely with her taking (finding/making) time to check back to ask if we were satisfied with the food she had cooked and served.

As an old HR person I recognized my obligation to let Chris know how impressed I was with her work and also asked if she was the owner or held any equity in the place. (Why else would anyone work so hard?) She was appreciative of the compliment, advised that she was only an employee, not an owner, and that I should come back again when her boss was on shift because her boss was twice as fast and a much better cook. I think you call that leadership by example. The service could not have been better if a dozen employees worked at the lodge. I was deeply impressed.

The second impressive worker that I witnessed in action happened the next morning when we met with the outfitter's wife, Annette. She happened to hold down a full time job to help support their family plus she handled all the administrative and logistical support for the outfitter organization. I was also told that she was an excellent hunter in her own right and could easily work as a registered and licensed guide. Her husband was in the field with clients at this time as it was already the second week of the hunting season, consequently all the administrative work for the business fell on her shoulders. This was Saturday and Annette's "day off".

On her day off she was up at 4:30 a.m. to prepare for a two-hour drive to "power shop" for the next group of hunters. All the food for the hunting parties, the working staff, horses and mules had to be flown in, and she had to buy everything and make all flight arrangements to get things into the various hunting camps correctly and on time. After completing the power shopping, which filled the back of a Ford F-350 pick-up truck, she then had to pick up two newly arrived hunters at the airport and make the return drive. At that time she had to meet with all five new hunting clients, complete licensing and administrative work for each of the five, and coordinate the flight logistics to start each hunter's highly anticipated adventure. She did everything with a smile and grace, including a very difficult communications obligation --- Annette had to advise all five anxious hunters that they would not be able to fly out on their respective hunts due to poor flight conditions (not what any of these hunters wanted to hear). She then hastened to find suitable overnight lodging for everyone. Annette was simply an amazing worker and a delightful individual to work with.

GENDER WORK CHANGES

It is my firm belief and professional opinion that female workers represent the greatest new human asset that has been given to American business. Females are a relatively new human asset because social tradition and past business practices have excluded females from many occupations and careers. I say this because it is simply true.

I remember one of my high school yearbooks had two pages in the center of the book (centerfold, I guess) where boys were pictured on one page and girls on the opposite page. The heading at the top of the "boy" page read: "Boys prepare for careers" and showed a kid working a slide rule in math class (no handheld calculators back then) and some shop boys welding and working on cars, ostensibly preparing themselves for the world of work. The heading at the top of the "girl" page read: "and girls prepare for modern homemaking" with pictures below of girls in what we called home economics class; cooking, sewing and ironing clothes. It was a clear social message, men worked and women stayed home. It was the conforming social expectation of the time. Some readers may remember that back in those days girls were also expected to make their own prom dresses! May sound crazy but that was the well entrenched way things worked back in the late 50s and into the early 60s. My work as a personnel manager/human resource vice president dated back well into the days when we ran help wanted advertisements for men only and other help wanted ads that were for women only (some newspapers continued this practice into the early 1980s). Women, of course, were generally relegated to lower pay jobs with little or no authority or responsibility.

Some managers also had a habit of "cooking-up" unrealistic job lifting and strength requirements designed primarily to exclude women from manufacturing jobs. In Chapter 15 this issue will be covered in more detail but let me share with you two stories that may help debunk that old management bias:

This first story is about an experience I had with a female who was incredibly strong. This is a true story and the names have only been changed to protect the guilty. The incident took place before I worked in the steel mill and I was the plant personnel manager for a large manufacturing shop that worked a five-day, three-shift, twenty-four hour operation. I came to work one Monday morning and noticed what I first thought was red paint thrown all over the parking lot and up against the wall of the building near the plant entrance. The red was everywhere, and on closer examination the red seemed to be too thin for paint. After going into my office I asked our plant nurse to look at the red in the lot and tell me if she thought it might be blood. She came right back into my office and advised that it was definitely blood and if all that blood came from one person, the person could not possibly be alive. Blood was splattered everywhere, and on closer examination it looked like a torture scene out of a Russian KGB movie. No one on day shift seemed to know what had happened, however I soon found out that it involved two of our second shift workers at the end of their shift on Friday evening (some of the strangest things occur on night shift).

Here's what happened: A plant worker on second shift (I'll call him Gus) though married with four children, also had a girlfriend (I'll call her Hilda) who did not work at the plant. Hilda was four months pregnant by Gus. Gus also had a newly acquired second girlfriend (I'll call her Sara) who worked with him on the second shift. Gus was a guy who either needed an immense amount of female attention or was an outright masochist. It seems that Hilda found out about Sara and became rather upset. It apparently didn't bother Hilda that Gus was married with four kids, but he was doing her wrong when he took on Sara as an additional girl friend. Hilda waited in the company parking lot for Gus and Sara to leave the plant at the end of their shift on Friday evening. When Hilda saw Gus walking hand in hand with Sara, she lost control, attacked both of them, and proceeded to pound them into the parking lot pavement. One male worker exiting the plant tried to break up the fight. Hilda quickly knocked him to the ground. When he started to get up, she picked him up by the nap of the neck and seat of his pants, and threw him head first into a parked car. This left a giant dent in the passenger-side door of the parked car and the helpful employee knocked nearly unconscious. Hilda then continued to beat on both Gus and Sara without mercy, repeatedly knocking them to the ground and alternately throwing both head first into the brick wall near the plant entrance (she must have determined that the side of a parked car was too soft for these two-timers).

Other second shift employees watching this fracas were hesitant to interfere after seeing the first person who tried to break up the fight get thrown head first into a parked car. Plus, one of the bystanders later told me that even though he felt sorry for Sara, everyone thought Gus was getting what he deserved and actually enjoyed seeing him get slammed around the parking lot. Reportedly, a few bystanders were cheering Hilda on, only adding to the dilemma by pumping up her adrenalin (Gus had a few enemies). This was clearly a one-person massacre. Hilda eventually tired, and with the help of the police and some of the bystanders, this one-sided fight was brought to a close. I tell you Hilda was one strong woman.

The following Monday, Gus came to see me in my office leading Sara by the hand. Gus's face was badly beaten and swollen, plus the thumb on his right had was pulled out of place and was sticking straight up. Sara took off the large dark sun glasses that she was wearing, and her eyes had been beaten completely shut. Now, remember this was Monday morning, and the altercation occurred on Friday night. I have never seen two people beaten so horribly, it was a gruesome sight. Now, get this: Neither Gus nor Sara had yet gone for any professional medical attention because they wanted to wait for Monday morning and have me put them onto workers compensation for their injuries!

I immediately directed them to the local clinic and advised both Gus and Sara that their injuries were not work-related and would not be covered under the workers compensation program. (Note: In Ohio's lop-sided workers compensation program, my decision on this matter could have easily been reversed by a State hearing officer.) You will read more on State Workers Compensation in Chapter 15.

Story number two involved some fun I experienced while working in the Steel Mill. My human resource/ personnel job at the mill included responsibility for periodic plant tours. I loved doing this because the steel making process was impressive and these tours got me out into the manufacturing operation where HR people must be visible.

At one job station the worker (called chainman) stood on a raised platform at the end of a bar mill. The large diameter steel bars exited this mill, were cut to size and cradled in a monstrous rack adjacent to the chainman's platform before being transferred to the next work site. Moving steel about the mill was handled using overhead cranes and electro magnets but this bar-mill presented problems as the steel was red hot and electro magnets cannot safely pick up red hot steel. Once the hot steel was cradled, the chainman had to physically throw huge chains beneath the cradle. These chains, not magnets, were then be used by the overhead crane to pick up and move the steel to the next work location.

Watching the chainman do this work always held touring guests in awe. The chains used were large diameter heavy monsters and had to be thrown by hand a considerable distance landing on the floor of the mill with a loud boom. Just seeing the chainman in action caused tour participants to believe they just witnessed a world-class strongman finish an impossible physical feat.

Now one of the chainmen just happened to be an attractive young lady of average build with blonde hair flowing from below her hard hat.

I did my level best to arrange plant tours at times she was scheduled to work. Tour participants were shocked beyond belief and this young lady loved putting on a show --- it was great fun!

You see what this chainman (woman) knew was the job required more technique than physical strength. The huge chain could be gathered up in sections at the end of the working platform, allowed to swing below the platform while holding onto the right chain links and stepping forward (like rolling a bowling ball) --- the momentum of the chain helped to propel it the distance required. Yes, the job was hot, dirty, noisy, intimidating and it did require some physical prowess but not the power of King Kong or The Green Hulk to get it done.

Read more on physical testing in Chapter 15.

I was part of the culture that restricted opportunities for women and am happy to see the profound new change in management attitudes regarding women working at all levels of an organization. Positions in all disciplines; be it sales, manufacturing, engineering, or at the top executive level are being preformed today by women in magnificent fashion. Opening that closed door was a talent blessing for business because well educated, highly motivated women were then given new work/career opportunities where they previously had never been considered.

There were some "adjustment" issues that needed to be addressed as this change started to take place. Namely, getting some men to accept women as working equals was, at times, a task, and sexual harassment issues surfaced on a regular basis. To shut this unacceptable practice down, management had to enforce strong disciplinary measures. Employment termination (industrial capital punishment) often resulted. I will share with you two stories.

Story number one took place in the large steel mill where I worked as HR manager in the late 1970s. Nearly three-thousand people were employed at this location and it worked a twenty-four hour schedule, seven days a week, with plant workers exiting the plant at the same time other workers were arriving. Manufacturing workers used a time clock to "punch-in" and "punch-out". To maintain order in the clock house with so many people moving in and out at the same time, separate lines were set up for departing and arriving workers. Each person picked up a time card in a rack (in or out), punched the clock and then deposited the time card in the next rack (in or out). These time clocks and card racks were situated back-to-back so the workers would pass by one another going in opposite directions.

One female worker was a voluptuous woman who I would describe as physically "top-heavy," and she liked to display this physical attribute by wearing tight-fitting upper garments. While this did not represent standard mill attire, it was not indecent nor was it unsafe . . . a distraction for some yes, but not cause for management concern.

As she entered the plant one day, through the clock house, a male employee passing in the opposite direction, reached over and grabbed her firmly by one of her breasts. Only God knows what was going through this numbskull's mind, but his offensive action caused the woman to rightfully scream in indignation. It resulted in a very ugly scene in the clock house, his arrest by plant security, and termination preliminary to discharge by management.

What stupefied me was this character's straightforward defense for his actions. In a formal disciplinary meeting with third party (union) representation he expressed indignation that he should be slapped with such harsh punishment and said: *"It was just a friendly hello!"*

That "friendly hello" landed him in the unemployment office. Now, anytime I see a woman built and dressed like her, his stupid words return to mind . . . "just a friendly hello!"

Story number two actually took place in Japan. I was working with a Japanese manager here in the USA, and like most Japanese managers/ directors, he was very bright, loyal to the company, and a good person to work with. He had been working in the USA a number of years and was called back to Tokyo for a business meeting. On this visit to Japan the guy just mysteriously disappeared, leaving his office and personal belongings behind. He abruptly vanished from the radar screen. It was several weeks before I found out what happened to him.

In the manager's absence from Japan, some changes had taken place regarding women's rights. One change involved a practice of touching females in public. In Japan it was not deemed inappropriate for a male to touch a female stranger without consent in public. A complementary pat on the back side or a pat elsewhere was okay. Incredulous maybe, but I understood this public touching was an accepted past practice.

Unfortunately, my manager friend was not aware that in his absence the women's rights movement in Japan managed to put an end to that formally accepted social custom. On a subway ride into Tokyo he reportedly, and unwittingly, touched an attractive young lady in a way she deemed inappropriate. The second unfortunate circumstance for him on this train ride was that the young lady he touched happened to be very active in the women's rights movement and served that organization in some official capacity. The scene got ugly. I later learned that it involved the police, his arrest, it made headlines in Tokyo newspapers, and worst of all caused enormous embarrassment to my manager friend.

To this day I do not know what ultimately happened to the guy. He just vaporized as though he had been shot into a cosmic black hole. One thing I do know is that he lost his job, falling victim to what some might consider *"Just a friendly hello."*

Some other work-related sexual harassment encounters come to mind but most of those were not at all humorous. Sexual harassment at the work site is a serious matter and business leaders need to be prepared to take appropriate action to remedy any and all abuses.

CHAPTER 10

SECOND HUNTING DAY
(CONTINGENCY PLANNING IN THE LAST FRONTIER)

My second hunting day appeared to be more complicated than the first with adverse weather that included rain, high winds, and low atmospheric ceilings. Seeing the leaves blowing wildly on deciduous trees did not trouble me, however watching the conifers blow sharply from side to side was not a comforting sight. While disappointed, I was getting myself prepared to accept another one-day delay.

We met with our pilot, Lance Williams, and were encouraged when he advised that a flight might be doable if we would drive to a second airport (or airstrip) that was located forty or so miles north. This location had reported milder wind conditions and better visibility. Lance arranged to pick us up there, and he was 100 percent correct about the flight conditions. While the weather on this day was somewhat marginal, our flight conditions at altitude proved to be very good, and I enjoyed a smooth ride over the mountains in the remarkable Piper Super Cub. I absolutely loved these old "rag and tube" Pipers. This particular Cub was just a little rough looking on the outside with the oversize tires and some well worn paint clinging to its fabric covering. The covering was why pilots referred to these airplanes as rag and tube. They had a steel tube structure or frame with a fabric called ceconite stretched over the frame of the fuselage and the wings. This manufacturing technique kept the airplane very light yet preserved the structural integrity needed for flight. This particular Cub was powered by a four cylinder opposed, Lycoming O 320 engine of 160 HP, a truly fine old power plant. Attached to the undercarriage of the fuselage were those two enormous "tundra" tires that were designed to roll over rocks and other obstacles that would allow landings in very remote areas.

I watched as Lance met with one hunter a day earlier at the airport in town. This hunter had his gear unloaded on the airport tarmac ready for a flight that due to poor weather would not take place. As Lance looked at, then picked up the hunter's gear, he grimaced, shook his head, and told the hunter that his gear was much too heavy and would require two separate flights to get him and his gear flown into the hunting camp of his destination. Otherwise, the hunter might want to go through his gear and remove some things that might be unnecessary. This hunter was clearly well over the seventy pound maximum, as he had two very large duffle bags stuffed full, plus an extra bag that he brought along that also appeared heavy by the way the pilot picked it up. Lance was so good at weight distribution in his airplane that it seemed he could casually look at the hunter and his gear, from a distance, and know the weight without the use of a scale or even taking time to lift the bags.

I actually found the seventy-pound hunting-gear limit easy to meet and yet I still carried more spare clothing than I would need or use. I also knew that the flight into my hunting area was the longest and crossed some very high peaks in the Alaska Range, so the pilot would be extra concerned about the weight of my gear. My bags were ready to load, and after completing his pre-flight check on the Piper Cub, Lance walked to the starboard side where my bags sat. I pointed to the first bag telling him, "That one weighs twenty-six and a half pounds, this second one weighs eighteen pounds, I have a couple things in my backpack, and my rifle that I can carry on my lap."

He looked at me, smiled, and said, "I really like how you pack!"

When loading my bags I could tell that Lance was both thorough and careful with every single item he placed on board (a Super Cub had limits) even checking my rifle to make sure that it was unloaded. A rifle discharging in a Cub could be dangerous and truly life threatening, not just from the threat of getting shot. For weight distribution reasons, there are two fuel tanks on this Piper that are located in the wings at the wing root close to the fuselage and a third fuel tank sat at the bottom of the fuselage directly beneath the passenger and pilot. One careless rifle discharge and the Piper, pilot, and passenger might disintegrate into a ball of flame before ever hitting the ground.

The flight to my base camp covered land that was truly spectacular. The rugged mountains, deep valleys, and beautiful streams all feeding the river drainage were incredibly impressive sights. Each mountain had its own monumental character, each stream cut its own unique trail down the mountain - over waterfalls and through the forest, plus the physical expanse was awesome. Lance and I were perched in our own little airplane world with a spectacular view of everything below.

Landing at the remote airport was an exhilarating experience. This airport was no more than a short stretch of gravel on the side of a mountain ridge that years ago had been used to support some type of mining exploration. It was slightly uphill and on some days, depending on the wind, was a one-way-in and one-way-out special with a few large rocks on the landing strip that would have presented a driving challenge to any Yuppie in an SUV.

Lance lined up for the landing, dropped flaps, side-slipped the Cub just a little, and we bounced in for what I can only call a perfect landing. God, I loved it! As a pilot, Lance was good, very good.

Piper Super Cub on tundra tires

When the Super Cub departed, I could not help being overwhelmed by the isolation. There I was standing in this great expanse of land, and my thoughts as the Cub disappeared into the horizon were simple. *This is it, you are here Bill, there are no roads, no cabins, no gas stations, and no restaurants . . .it's time to become part of the last frontier.* Jesus, it's a lonely feeling that I simply could not find words to describe. Nor can I accurately describe the great beauty of the land surrounding me, the tremendous distances, the fresh smell of the air, the majestic snow capped mountains, and the quiet, so very quiet surroundings. Robert Service said it best in this verse from his poem "Spell of the Yukon:"

> *"It's the great, big, broad land 'way up yonder,*
> *It's the forests where silence has lease:*
> *It's the beauty that thrills me with wonder,*
> *It's the stillness that fills me with peace."*

Here was truly the stillness that you could not find anywhere else on earth. For me there were no management meetings, no noise, no work chaos, there was only natural beauty, fresh smelling air and silence to behold. Clearly my journey had already secured tremendous rewards.

Meeting up with my hunting guide, unfortunately, was far less rewarding. All the months of preparation lead me to anticipate a more friendly and supportive camp setting. As it turned out the hunting base camp had just been moved and was set up adjacent to this air strip, and absent a hunter departing the area, no one present even bothered to say hello. After waiting thirty minutes or so, I approached two individuals sitting on the mountainside adjacent to this camp site, introduced myself, and asked if one of them would be my guide. They responded that they were both guides and said little more. This poor initial meeting would prove to be a harbinger of things to come.

In Alaska you could not hunt on the same day that you flew or rode in an airplane. It was a good rule that I could support as it eliminated the "fly & shoot" approach to hunting that I personally considered very unethical. So with no hunting to do, the rest of hunting day two was spent setting up a tent, storing my gear, and preparing for the first day out, even though my guide did not say a single word about what we would do, what I needed to have with me, or where and how we would hunt.

ALASKA HUNTING KNOWLEDGE

Part of my hunting preparation plan (goal) was to secure a copy of the summarized Alaska game laws given to hunters and potential hunters, so I could familiarize myself with the rules and regulations for the game management area where I planned to hunt. My Fairbanks Army buddy was kind enough to send me a copy of the official ADF&G booklet that explained Alaska's hunting and fishing regulations. Now, hunting regulation booklets are only designed to be a brief summary of the game laws as the actual hunting regulations embrace many volumes that I am sure would, alone, have exceed my seventy-pound gear limit for the hunt.

Each state issued an annual summary of game regulations to hunters that was designed and written to briefly describe the state game laws and hunter requirements. In my home state I was given a small booklet that was approximately five by seven inches in size that could easily be folded in half to will fit nicely into a shirt pocket. The brief game law summary from ADF&G however was a bit different. This baby took on the form of a legal and zoological encyclopedia. A 112 page, 8 ½ by 11 inch monster that upon examination I found difficult to follow and more than just a tad complex.

The state of Alaska covered an enormous geographical expanse and was divided into twenty-six separate game management areas. Several of those game management areas were sub-divided into other areas and each area and/or subdivision could have very different hunting regulations. Additionally, identifying the geographical boundaries described for these various regulated hunting areas would be a challenge for even the best civil engineer. You truly needed to know precisely where you were standing before you took a shot at any game animal in Alaska. Even some of the basic rules established by the ADF&G for various management areas could be rather complex.

I was to be hunting in an area that only allowed hunting bull moose (no cows) and had the added requirement that out-of-state (or alien) hunters determine that the bull had an antler spread of at least fifty inches before shooting. Now even though I had never hunted a moose, I knew that any bull moose with an antler spread of fifty inches was a monster, and I also knew that these monsters could be very dangerous and cantankerous beasts. I couldn't imagine one standing still while I pulled out a tape measure to determine the size of the antlers on it's head. Thank you ADF&G.

Here's another gem taken from this booklet: If you were hunting sheep in this game management area you could only shoot a ram. Now before you shot a ram you were obligated to determine that the ram had at least one antler/horn that curled to 270 degrees or greater. Per the ADG&G I guess you needed to add a protractor to your hunting gear. Other seasoned hunters I met in Alaska cautioned me that the ADF&G was very serious about these requirements, and it was doomsday for anyone shooting a moose that was only forty-nine inches or a ram with a curl of only 265 degrees.

And my favorite: If you were hunting caribou in this game area you were restricted to hunting only bulls. Caution here as this gets dicey, because both male and female (bulls & cows) have antlers. Do not fear, the ADF&G provided you with some remarkable guidance in determining the sex of a caribou in the wild. Per the ADF&G, here is the number one way to do this <u>and I quote this exactly as it is printed in the ADF&G 2006 – 2007 Alaska Hunting Regulations Book.</u> "The best method to identify bulls is to determine the presence of a penis sheath." Incredible but true. If hunters adhered to the letter of that law, I suspected many caribou had been left prancing around the woods with bullets in their backsides.

To hunt with a tape measure, well maybe but not likely, to hunt with a protractor, well maybe but not likely. . . . hunt caribou, NOT LIKELY!

> *"I don't make jokes; I just watch*
> *the government and report the facts"*
>
> *Will Rogers*

My experience in the manufacturing business taught me that if you had people employed in your organization who had work time available to cook up complex, over-detailed rules and witless advice like some of the material I read in this ADF&G legal/zoological encyclopedia, it can only mean that there was a serious over staffing problem present in the organization. Sorry ADF&G, I have to call 'em as I see 'em.

Third Hunting Day

There were two hunters sent into this base camp, a seasoned big game hunter from Nebraska and me. We were to meet with our guides at base camp and then start our respective hunts. In the base camp there were three men working who were employed as guides (actually two guides and one packer). All three of these individuals had been born and raised in a Southern state that many in the north describe as being rather backward or even unenlightened. I will not make that generalization, but if I based judgments solely on initial impressions, my thoughts would add credibility to that northern bias. This trio of tarnished characters had been living in the woods without shave or shower for the last month, but their appearance reflected a much longer stay. No big deal to me, I hadn't traveled this great distance for a class in sanitation and hygiene; I came to hunt moose.

The senior member of this threesome, and the leader of the pack, Ed (not his real name) was a registered/licensed Alaska hunting guide. The second in line, Joe, (not his name either) was also a registered/licensed guide. The guide assigned to me was a young man in his early twenties who spoke very little. His name was Charlie (fake name as well), and I found his guiding assistance to be more than mildly disappointing. As I found out later, the outfitter I signed up with subcontracted some of his guide work to other hunting guides, including these three individuals as he was booked solid with other hunters throughout the hunting season. Charlie was not an employee of the outfitter, and I later determined him to be a guide who clearly fell near the bottom of that group representing seventy-five percent of registered guides referenced earlier. Actually I was not able to find Charlie even listed as a registered guide when I returned home and checked the registry connected to the ADF&G Web site.

I explained to Charlie that I was sixty-one years old and my large game hunting experience had been in Ohio and Pennsylvania pursuing whitetail deer. This was my first moose hunt, actually my first guided big game hunt, and I was anxious to learn as much as possible about moose hunting. I also wanted to learn about other animals living in the area and would like to hear about any interesting hunting experiences he had had and would be willing to share.

The quote by Henry Ford is right about learning new things and Charlie, while young, certainly had hunting knowledge and experience beyond mine that, as my guide, he could and should have shared with me.

It is also important to note that I never dismiss youth when it comes to job knowledge. As example, my pilot was a very young man who I found to be a truly superior pilot. He took time when we were together to teach me a few things about mountain flying, and I can say without qualification that mountain flying demands strong aviation piloting skills and requires experience far greater than I possess as a pilot. I sincerely appreciated him taking time on our flights to share with me some of his vast flying knowledge . . . you see, to me, this pilot was an aviation guide. I anticipated that my hunting time with Charlie would prove to be a valuable learning experience as well. Unfortunately this was a misplaced anticipation.

HUNTING MOOSE

There were basically three ways to hunt moose; floating, calling, and glassing. Floating required the use of a river boat or raft (and pliable waterways) to carry the hunter through a selected hunting area. I had never hunted from a boat or raft, however my Alaska hunt later provided opportunities for me to meet with some raft hunters and I discovered that the floating method for hunting moose is anything but easy.

The calling method of hunting came to the fore during the rutting season when bulls were seeking mates and out to protect their territory. This method worked best in late September and October when the rut was in full swing. I've read stories about hunters using the calling technique for moose and found it interesting what bizarre things moose will do when they are deceived by a fake call during the rutting season. Some moose had actually stalked then charged at hunters who were calling them. One bull reportedly roared directly into a hunting base camp, surprising hunters who were sitting by their camp fire practicing moose calling techniques (those guys must have been good).

The glassing method required a good pair of binoculars and a ton of patience. A hunter using this method needed to be positioned where he/she could overlook a basin, valley, or mountainside to view moose at a distance using high power binoculars. Most importantly the hunter needed to be very quiet, be positioned downwind, and remain unseen. Moose are large animals but could be very difficult to see when bedded down and not moving about. Big as they are, moose blended into the boreal forest so well that they appeared to be invisible.

A human dilemma also existed when hunting moose. Humans, naturally and automatically, have placed wild animals into our human living environment. Humans are diurnal animals. Consequently we hunt deer (a moose is a big deer – big deer) during the day when our human eyes and body operate best and could be oblivious to the fact that most deer live nocturnally. Their eyes accepted more light at night and they are not only comfortable traveling at night, they preferred to move about after dark. The impression I had regarding moose viewed on my hunt was that they acted in a more crepuscular way. They came out at dusk to eat and move about and then would bed down, moving again in the early morning twilight hours. Regardless, the dilemma here was that we human hunters spend a ton of time hunting animals on our human terms when those animals were just not present to be hunted.

Once years ago I was in Denali Park near a small stream, and I was convinced this steam held some catchable fish (artic grayling). The area was treeless and wide open; you could see for miles. I scanned the entire stretch of this stream from the mountainside I was on and saw nothing that would cause danger or alarm, so I took my seven-year-old son with me and started working this stream with a fly rod. As I said, the area was very open and so flat that it appeared difficult for even a small ground squirrel to find adequate camouflage and cover. However after walking the stream and fishing for about a quarter of a mile we managed to walk right up on a resting bull caribou. He was a fully mature bull, and his gigantic antlers were in full velvet. This bull was so close that I could have easily used the ADF&G method to determine his sex. The bull was lying down when I approached, and as he stood up I could have touched him with the end of my fishing rod. I was frozen stiff with my small son right behind me and this big bull right in front, but there was absolutely nothing I could do. The bull did not move. It was an agonizing standoff. I remember looking into the bull's dark eyes and telling him, "Hey, it's your call pal." There wasn't even a small rock or stick anywhere near to use for defense, and the fishing rod I held in my hand was as useless as that plastic Smithsonian Star Finder. The standoff seemed to take an eternity until the bull finally decided it was time to leave, turned and trotted away while looking back at me the entire time to see what I was doing. With my heart pounding like a jackhammer I grabbed my son's hand and made it directly back to the high ground and relative safety. What bothered me most at that time and continues to bother me now as I reflect back on it is that a very large brown bear could have easily hidden in that same shallow depression. A brown bear would have been even more difficult to see than a caribou with massive antlers, and I fearfully doubt that a startled bear would have elected to simply trot away as did this caribou. Wild animals blend into their surroundings so naturally, and wild animals are, well . . . wild!

So close I could touch him with my fishing rod

Hunting using the glassing method could be strenuous as you were looking for anything small that might give away an animal's location, a slight color variation, a flash of an antler, or some type of movement. Even though moose are the largest game animals in North America, glassing for one standing still in the boreal forest is like looking for that proverbial needle in a hay stack.

It was the second week of September which made it too early for the full rutting season and use of the calling method. Since I was not using a river raft for transportation, the glassing method would be my modus operandi.

OFF ON FOOT

Before departing we ate breakfast in the guide's tent, and the meal was an interesting experience. I recognized that you must never expect too much in the way of culinary care coming from any moose camp, or you would be disappointed. Despite that recognition, I remembered looking at the outfitter's web page before departing, where one photograph displayed a complete table arrangement with what appeared to be king crab legs placed on each plate. Being a seafood addict, that table fair looked just fine by me, even though I did not truthfully expect to be served king crab while hunting so far back into the last frontier. I didn't travel that monumental distance to sample culinary delicacies - I was there to hunt. I found out later there was an ample supply of food in the base camp, not king crab, but more food than would be needed by the hunters and guides, regardless of their appetite. On this morning it was the food preparation that was unique, to say the least. Breakfast was sausage, eggs, and coffee (the bread supply had mysteriously vanished), with Ed doing the cooking. The food prepared by Ed was okay even though all he had in camp to cook with was one small pot, two seldom cleaned frying pans, a spatula, four forks (there were five guys in this camp), five spoons, four coffee cups, and a beat-to-hell, wired-together container that at one time might have resembled a coffee pot. All the cooking was done on a single antique Coleman stove that had long since exceeded its serviceable life. Dinning out with this crew was an interesting experience but, for the most part, food was acceptable, bacteria be damned.

There were twelve animals (horses and mules) in this base camp, however Charlie advised that we would not be using horses and would proceed on foot. I can only wonder why the oldest person in the hunting camp (me) was sent out on this first day to cover the longest distance on foot. We headed off in a westerly direction to find a good spot to glass for moose. The two guides present at base camp, Ed and Joe, mounted horses with the other hunter in camp and headed off in a northerly direction across the adjacent river pulling the string of mules.

Physically, I felt very prepared for this hunt as I had spent months at a local gym building up my strength and endurance. For additional training I put on a fully loaded backpack, slung a rifle over my shoulder, hung binoculars around my neck, and then ran up and down stairs to build up my legs and back. The terrain we covered on that day however really took a toll on my knees. Climbing rocky mountains, jogging on relatively flat land, and running stairwells was significantly different from what I experienced on that cross-country march. The forests were appreciably thick with soft uneven footing. The swamps held deep muck that pulled on every step. The tundra was a hidden marsh of its own, and the mountains that looked so smooth from a distance had a surface of uneven, soft, spongy moss layers that challenged every step. The difficulty for a human knee in this terrain was that your foot became fixed in place and your knee was called on to move in unnatural directions. The good doctor Feldstein would advise you that a hip could take this side-twisting motion but knees could not.

Charlie was not very talkative and said so little, in fact, you could count on one hand the words he said from the time we departed base camp. He was certainly physically conditioned to travel through this difficult terrain and maintained a strong pace. For me it was a different story. While I felt very prepared and considered myself to be in excellent condition for my hunt I was clearly not able to maintain a pace equal to Charlie's. My mistake right at the front was to do everything possible to keep up even though there was no need to hurry, and I personally believed that a slower pace would have been a much better hunting posture. My body's cardiopulmonary functions held up fine, however my knees started to send me messages that they were being pushed too hard. I elected to ignore those messages and would pay a price.

We had been traveling on foot for more than three hours, and I started calling out to Charlie asking that he slow down, but my words seemed to be falling on deaf ears. If anything Charlie went faster with each request to slow the pace and was constantly out of sight. I was very frustrated, as I paid a significant sum of money to have a guided hunt and I ended up with a guide who turned a deaf ear to my requests and was constantly out of sight.

"If you come to a fork in the road, take it."

Attributed to Yogi Berra

It appeared that Charlie really didn't know where he was going. It was a case of the blind leading the blind. He was an experienced woodsman, but I didn't believe he ever hunted in that particular neck of the woods and was actually stumbling through the woods trying to figure out where we should be headed. There were a number of times that we backtracked and circled around as Charlie worked to find his way. The backtracking did slow Charlie down and provided an opportunity for me to locate him and then catch up.

The distance traveled straight and circular was taking a toll on my knees as well as my patience, however we eventually ended up on a ridgeline at 3400 feet altitude (per my GPS) that overlooked a river valley and appeared to be a good spot to glass for moose. Charlie suggested that I stay on this first ridge and pointed to a second adjacent ridge where he said he would set up to glass the valley and cover more area. This was okay by me as I was beat, and the second ridge required more walking through difficult terrain. Charlie also said that we would use some hand signals to communicate. They were basically: 1. Both hands out with fingers up meant that I saw a bull. 2. Both hands out and fingers down meant that I saw a moose but it was a cow. 3. Four fingers up on one hand meant that the bull had four brow tines (four brow tines made the bull legal quarry).

This was great by me as I finally received a little guidance from my guide, and the arrangements seemed to make sense. The distance between the ridges was significant, but we would be able to see one another and the signals should work fine. My big question was how to stalk a sighted bull so far down in this valley when we were perched at 3400 feet. That question could be answered later, the first job was to spot the bull.

I watched as Charlie made his way to the second ridge, we waved to one another, he turned, went out of sight and I did not see him again for over four hours. I had no idea what my guide was doing, and I had no idea why we had established a visual hand signal arrangement when Charlie immediately elected to disappear. But hey, my knees needed a rest, and the topography of the area was utterly fantastic. Somehow we managed to stumble onto a magnificent geographical setting that was deep into "The last frontier," and the sights were breathtaking.

Glassing perch at 3400 MSL

I not only glassed for moose, I glassed the mountains from their snow covered tops to the alluvial fans at their base. I watched birds in flight, otters in the lakes, and mountain goats on a rocky slope miles away. High in the sky were F-15's fighter jets in flight and I am confident that they were the same jets that I saw on my tour of Elemdorf Air Force Base in Anchorage. Those F-15's (Orions of Earth's airspace) were obviously out practicing their hunting skills. It was an unseasonably warm day, and I was enjoying every minute.

The Last Frontier

The winds were acutely strong, coming directly out of the southwest, and it did not take long for a rainstorm to materialize. The dark clouds could be seen at a great distance working through and over the mountains, and the sheets of rain were on the way, clearly visible. I quickly donned my rain gear, then climbed beneath a rock ledge to have some lunch. Incredibly the rain rapidly turned to snow and then back to rain. Weather in the Alaska mountain range can change fast and you must always be prepared for any adverse conditions. My well-prepared hunting attire worked flawlessly keeping me warm and dry.

Charlie eventually appeared on the ridge holding up a shed antler from a caribou. He seemed to be trying to get my attention and kept waving and pointing to the antler. No hand signals were used, so I figured he must have seen a herd of caribou and wanted me to join him on the second ridge for a look. It took some time to reach that ridge and as it turned out Charlie had seen two bull moose in the valley below (no caribou). I asked about the caribou antler and why he abandoned the hand signals that we agreed to use, but he was busy setting up his spotting scope to get a better view of the bulls and ignored my questions. It was near dark now, and watching Charlie it was clear he knew a few things about hunting moose. He was very excited about spotting the bulls and was intensely focused on tracking their every move. I spotted two additional bulls and soon saw a total of six bulls in the valley below. Three of the bulls I watched were beginning to posture for the rutting season and engaged antlers for some pushing contests with each other. It was exciting to watch them from the ridge as it was the type of animal interaction that you would see staged in an outdoor adventure movie, but this ridge and valley was not a stage; it was real.

Darkness was setting in, and Charlie said with conviction that an early morning hunt would produce a good shot at one of these bulls, as they would not move far. They would soon bed down and remain in this general area through tomorrow morning.

Valley with six bulls

We started back to base camp although the darkness made travel through the rugged terrain even more difficult. Here too Charlie refused to stay in sight, and I simply could not understand his indifference toward my repeated requests. I began to think that it was Charlie's goal to get me lost which was certainly not what I expected when I paid for a guided hunt. As I looked back on this situation, Charlie may have been in an unfamiliar area simply having problems with his woods navigation. We eventually found a creek that we followed in hopes that it would lead us in the right direction. Charlie seemed to have doubts about the route this creek would take yet we walked the creek bed for over two miles. It was ever so difficult to keep moving forward with my battered knees stumbling over the smooth slippery rocks while pushing against a strong varying current. The winding nature of the creek took me into the water then back onto the shore numerous times. The creek widened in spots with shallow depths then it would narrow down, produce fast currents and increase the depth to above my waist.

The creek banks were thick with trees, some areas so thick that passage was not possible. When I was forced out of the water I had to climb the steep banks, travel into the now dark woods to circle around the impassible stretch of water and find my way back to the creek further down stream. I didn't suffer from nyctohylophobia but if I did this would have been the time and place where I would have been reduced to a screaming pile of shot nerves on the forest floor. It was dark, and the thick woods very intimidating.

My knees were pretty shot by this time, causing me to stumble on the slippery stones and fall a number of times. Twice I went into the water above my boots and was soaked from head to foot. I had pushed my old body beyond its limits. Charlie continued to travel ahead and out of sight. When I was able to catch up to him he would only shout, *"We have to get off this creek, the wolves run this creek at night."*

What an astonishing tidbit of knowledge, wolves are nocturnal hunters, gee what would I do without Charlie as a guide? The wolves could be heard howling nearby base camp the night before, and this area was notorious for having many of them. For comfort I kept telling myself that wolf attacks on humans are rare, but that didn't provide much solace. In July of that year there were three reported wolf attacks on humans in Alaska. One attack took place near the artic circle and two more on the Dalton highway, and all three attacks were made by a lone wolf. If it was true that wolves avoided humans, why was Charlie (who should know) acting so anxious and fearful?

Wolves can be vicious killers

Wolves are opportunists capable of killing a healthy mature moose, and a pack of wolves would have an easy time taking care of me. I was the injured animal in this pack of two, and I was the one being left behind. It's always the trailing animal that gets picked off first and I was that injured, trailing animal. The creek did eventually lead to a trail crossing over to where the base camp was located, however it was 11:30 pm when I made my final climb out of that creek. At this point I'd been traveling nonstop on foot for over three hours, and absent my falls, took only one brief break to drop my pack, take a drink of water, and then move on. It had been a very long demanding day. Charlie was at the trail, and as I approached I told him, "Hey Charlie, you're turning the hunt of a lifetime into the hunt from hell." I meant every word.

Wolves run through here at night

The next morning, on horseback, traveling that same creek there were fresh wolf tracks to be seen following my boot prints all along the creek. Knowing that a pack of wolves were tracking me was more than just unsettling. I'd had to deal with corporate wolves throughout my career, and frankly they never impressed me. But these wolves, late at night, tracking me down a creek bed in the boreal forest scared the hell out of me.

Wolves have proven themselves to be great hunters and can be vicious animals. One of the hunters I met on this hunt showed me the remains of a fully grown bull moose that had been killed by wolves.

Wolf killed adult bull moose

I have now added wolves to my list of predators to avoid whenever possible. Bears, sharks and wolves will always receive a wide birth from me at every opportunity.

CHAPTER 11

THE HUNT FROM HELL CONTINUES
(EVALUATE OPTIONS – TAKE ACTION)

When I reached my tent the night before I was totally exhausted, and every inch of my body was completely soaked. Keeping dry when moose hunting in Alaska was generally one of the most demanding problems but this wet was ridiculous. I discarded my wet clothes, climbed into my sleeping bag for what I thought would be a deep night's sleep. My injured legs delivered so much pain to my brain however that sleep was out of the question. It would not be possible for me to describe how disheartened I was at that time. The hunt was turning out to be everything I didn't want in a hunting adventure. Even with a heavy dose of aspirin I was unable to sleep well, and yet I was up at 6 a.m., dressed for hunting, and ready for that early morning hunt that Charlie said would be on tap for this day. My crippled knee status did not dampen my enthusiasm for the hunt.

I went to the guide tent, and all three guides were sleeping soundly. I called for Charlie and reminded him that we had agreed to hunt early today, but Charlie it turned out didn't like getting up early for anything, hunting included. He never intended to leave base camp early, and we did not depart that morning until 8:30 am.

Now I admit that I'm pretty much a city boy even though I live in Amish farm country, but when I go hunting or fishing early it is not 8:30 a.m. To me 8:30 a.m. is late in the day and those early morning moose had certainly finished their morning stroll through the woods where they were last seen.

One thing I can tell you about those three disheveled guides is that they were absolutely fearless when it came to germs and bacteria. Two of them, Joe and Charlie, had their own private coffee cups that they guarded and did not elect to share with anyone else. I cannot imagine anyone wanting to use those cups as they were filthy beyond description. Those two characters both liked to chew tobacco, and in addition to using their cups for coffee, they would occasionally use the cups to deposit tobacco spittle. The cups were stained inside and out with that disgusting brown tarnish from the tobacco. On this morning I watched Joe prepare his morning coffee. He picked his coffee cup up off the floor of the tent and made an attempt to clear out the tobacco spittle coagulating on the inside by holding it upside down and banging it on the side of the camp stove. He then opened a package of powdered hot chocolate and emptied its contents into the cup. Following that he poured in hot coffee, drew his hunting knife from a sheath on his belt, and used it to stir the concoction.

I had never in my life seen anything like this and was mesmerized by his actions. Joe saw that my eyes were fixed on what he was doing. He looked at me, smiled, laughed, and said that he was just making his morning "Cowboy Latte." Joe was a character, and I couldn't help laughing with him. Heck, I suppose if you carved out the tobacco spittle and dirty hunting knife the beverage might be the same thing you would pay five dollars or more for at a Starbucks coffee shop.

I told Charlie that this had to be an early-morning hunt and that I wanted to check to see if the moose were stationed where we left them. I said I had no interest going that far into the woods to remain there late into the evening. My knees needed some rest and night travel through this uneven terrain would do them no good. In truth I had lost all confidence in Charlie but wanted to give him an opportunity to prove that he was a knowledgeable moose hunter and was right about the whereabouts of the bulls we glassed the night before.

We were riding horses on hunting day number four, and while I was definitely no equestrian and had minimal riding skill, I knew that I would do just fine. I also purchased some knicker treats (horse candy) at the country farm cooperative feed store in town before departing home. My horse was no prize winning steed but was a gentle animal and easy to ride. This horse also loved the knicker treats, and I deeply appreciated my four legged friend because every step that horse took was one that my beat old knees did not have to take. I had a walking stick with me that I made in camp that morning (utilizing the time available waiting for the early hunt to start) that would prove to be a tremendous aid. I would not have finished the hunt without it. That walking stick earned a permanent resting spot in my den and became my foremost trophy from this hunt from hell.

We rode our horses through the woods and then up the same creek that I had struggled to navigate on foot the night before. Here, unsettling as it was, I saw fresh wolf tracks encircling boot prints I had made in the sand. Twice we stopped, and I watched the horses while Charlie searched for a way through some of this rough thickly forested country. I was not sure if Charlie was looking for a route that would be easy on the horses (as he said), or if he was out there simply trying to figure out just where the hell we were. This ride was not a guide confidence builder for me.

Eventually we made our way out of the creek, through some woods, and into a clearing that Charlie said would be a good spot to tie off the horses. As we were dismounting our horses we spotted two bulls just off to our right side, out in the open, and both bulls were very big. I was amazed that the bulls did not bolt even though the wind was in our favor as we were very close and in plain view. They must have thought we looked like other moose or caribou as we rode out of the woods on our horses. Both bulls were slowly making their way toward a wooded area nearby as Charlie lead the way on our final stalk. It was truly exhilarating as the distance was close, and I began to think what a great way to end this hunt. My knees were continuing to send my brain those messages of grief, and I had lost all confidence and trust in my guide . . . Halleluiah, this hunt from hell would soon be over. I might even arrange an early flight out to get in some time fishing with my now retired old army pal in Fairbanks.

We moved behind cover on foot as best we could to get where a clear shot could be made. The bulls continued their move into the wooded area and were not in sight, however I sensed that they remained nearby. Charlie whispered that he would try a cow call to draw them out to get a better view of their antlers to make sure that both bulls were of legal size. Just after Charlie made two low volume cow moose grunts, three bull caribou bolted from the woods to our right. We had not seen the caribou and had no idea they were in the area. They were startled by the cow call or simply saw us or smelled us as the wind was changing now and now drifting in that direction. The three caribou charged directly up the mountain between the two bull moose and I. They were big bulls (using the ADF&G method to determine their sex was easy as the caribou ran away at an angle less than twenty yards to my right). Unfortunately the caribou startled the moose and the stalk was over. Charlie and I did continue the pursuit and tried to gain a ground advantage on the two bulls, but the bulls were aware that a problem was present and were soon out of sight.

Charlie decided that it would be best to continue on toward the ridge line that we used the night before and started off through the woods. Here too Charlie gave no direction and soon disappeared from sight. I had no idea where I was in the woods and the same guide-disappearing scenario started to unfold. I'd catch up to Charlie, ask him to at least try to keep me in sight, and then Charlie would disappear. I did not want to push my knees too hard by walking in circles through the rugged terrain we were covering, consequently I began a practice of stopping and waiting each time Charlie disappeared. I was pissed that this kid was absolutely refusing to be my guide. I paid for one, and what I received was profoundly unacceptable. Each time Charlie disappeared I called for him and then stood my ground to await his return. He would eventually reappear in the distance and the process started all over again . . . Charlie disappeared, I called and waited, eventually Charlie reappeared . . . over and over and over. I started to feel like the oppressed comedian Rodney Dangerfield when he told an audience, "My parents moved a lot when I was a kid, but I always found them."

It may have been that I was a little too naive at the onset of this hunt as I envisioned a more compatible hunter/guide arrangement. Maybe something like the old Lone Ranger TV Show where I would be the lone ranger, and my guide was the loyal Tonto at my side, giving directions. "This way Kemo Sabe. See tracks Kemo Sabe?" A vision that was certainly not too realistic.

This process ended when Charlie left me stranded in a heavily wooded area, and I stopped. Charlie was out of sight, but this time he did not return. I waited, then sat down, ate my lunch, and using my hunting knife managed to whittle some nice improvements to my walking stick. A considerable amount of time went by, maybe forty-five minutes or more. I was convinced that Charlie was gone for good this time. I also thought that he might have even taken a fall, injured himself and needed help. I decided to make some headway in a direction I thought Charlie might have taken and started calling for him. He suddenly appeared and was angry that I showed up making noise (calling for him), claiming that I had just scared away a moose. I was more angry with Charlie and told him that he was doing a shit job of guiding. Clearly this guide/hunter relationship was not going well and only getting worse.

Eventually we managed to find the ridge we were on the night before and took up positions to glass the valley. It was now early afternoon (not early morning) and there were no moose on the move. We didn't see them the prior night until nearly dark when they normally moved about, and I would not see them today as we would be back at base camp before nightfall.

I spent most of this afternoon glassing and thinking about how I would continue my hunt this week without a guide. My confidence in Charlie as a guide was at the zero mark, and if one of the other two guides at base camp were not available to work with me, then I would simply hunt by myself. Most of my deer hunting had been solo, and I could adapt to solo moose hunting with ease as long as my knees did not completely fail, plus my newly carved and enhanced walking stick was proving to be a very good support. I was already making my mental hunting plans for the next day but needed a good night's rest.

At around 6 pm. I walked the ridge to the area where Charlie had taken his position for glassing but he was gone (no surprise). I started calling for him as it was time to leave if we were to make it back to the horses before dark, but Charlie did not respond (again no surprise). I searched the ridge line from one end to the other and no Charlie.

Soon it would be dark, and I was fuming. I made repeated trips up and down the ridge, calling for my guide with no results. I decided that he was gone and to hell with him. I was prepared for a stay in the woods and had placed all the items I needed in my backpack, extra clothes, plenty of energy food, my GPS, compass, extra medicine and ammunition. . . . I was prepared (Scout Pack 222).

ARMY DAYS

As I mentally prepared to position myself for a night alone on the ground in the last frontier I had reason to reflect back on some of my old army days. I joined the army at age seventeen just a few months out of high school, and the nation was then at the peak of the Cold War with the Cuban missile crisis unfolding. Our military training was very thorough as we were all (trainers and trainees) convinced that we would need to face off with the Soviet Union at a moments notice. Physical and mental conditioning was important and our training exercises even after basic training (boot camp) included an exercise called infiltration and evasion. We were taken miles out into the woods or no man's land, often blindfolded, with only a compass, a map, and instructions to elude enemy aggressor forces and return to our bivouac area before dawn. Most guys hated this training, but I loved it, and I never once got caught. Using a compass for direction was second nature to me and shooting an azimuth a piece of cake. Military maps (on land called maps, in the air and sea called charts) also impressed me with their accuracy, attention to detail, and they were so easy to read. My choice was always to travel alone through the woods as groups made too much noise, drawing unwanted attention. I taught myself how to identify then avoid the obvious areas of entrapment. The army had a special way of making certain soldiers understood that the easy way was always mined. I moved in silence, never traveled the roads, avoided the traps and followed my compass direction. Also I didn't smoke cigarettes. Most GI's at that time smoked. Now you might think not smoking was no big deal when you were going through infiltration training, but it was a very big deal. After getting dropped off at night, the groups of GI's who were trying to get through the enemy aggressor forces always had smokers in their ranks, and someone would constantly light up at the wrong time. The noise made by those Zippo and Ronson lighters clicking open could be heard for great distances, plus the light from the cigarette was a beacon in the dark. Going through infiltration training made me wonder how many soldiers had lost their lives in combat because smoking cigarettes gave away their position.

I watched the noisy groups get captured by the aggressors and moved through the dark woods without capture. Once at Ft. Campbell, Kentucky, I had an opportunity to serve on an aggressor force for a field-training mission. We aggressors were given different uniforms and helmets and also were told that whatever our home country was, it did not honor the Geneva Convention and its rules for the humane treatment of prisoners. Our job was to capture and interrogate those infiltrating enemy soldiers, and we had a great time rounding them up by the dozen. We tied them to trees, temporarily stole their belongings, and hid their boots. My aggressor team was good, and we had fun. It was an experience I just never forgot.

Once on this aggressor mission I drove my jeep into our interrogation area holding two captive POW's tied together in the back. I happened to see that a soldier from my unit had an enemy officer (first lieutenant) staked, spread out on the ground like you would see in those old cowboy shows. I asked this guy if he thought he might be going a little too far with his interrogation as we were both just PFC's (privates). He responded in his best fake Russian: "Nada, Vee Vill get Zee Truth out of dis Amerikan Gangster."

He continued his interrogation and even threatened to kill the lieutenant with an M-79 grenade launcher. I unloaded the new captives, jumped back in my Jeep, and "got the hell out of Dodge." Fortunately the officer was a good guy, took the encounter in stride, and none of us ended up serving time in the brig.

As a side note, all the aggressor forces for this mission were selected from the 39th Combat Engineer Battalion and the enemy forces were all members of the elite 101st Airborne Division (fully airborne at that time). It was considered a disgrace for any member of the 101st to get captured in these training exercises, and to be captured by a bunch of engineers was an added insult! It was fun.

My Army reflections helped to assure me that I had the background training and education to do the things alone in the woods needed to survive (bin there, done that), and it was no big deal. I also knew how to hunt and hunt very well because I learned to hunt from the absolute best there was, my dad.

DECISION TIME

One of my father's favorite sayings was: "You make your bed, and you sleep in it." Well I guess that, unwittingly, I made this hunting guide mess and now needed to figure out how to make the most of it.

Standing on the ridge I thought about my options and while being resigned to accept a cold night on this mountain it was not my choice and had not been my plan for this day's hunt. My knees were in bad shape and my biggest concern. Both of them were in pain, beginning to swell, and a good night sleep in a warm sleeping bag was very much needed and foremost on my mind. Mentally, however, I was not able to overcome my anger regarding the unacceptable guide service I was getting and decided to fire one round from my rifle to get Charlie's attention, wherever he was.

This rifle had a loud rapport especially in the very quiet surrounding and yet the one round fired did not get my guide's attention, or he simply elected not to appear. Frustrated, I waited and fired three more rounds. Still no Charlie, so I started my preparations for a night's stay on the ridge when suddenly Charlie came forward. He had been sitting on the side of the ridge just below a rock outcropping, and I was fully convinced that he heard my vocal calls, searching for him and simply ignored me. He also heard my shots and as he approached asked if I had been the one doing that shooting. I replied, "Who the hell do you think it was? There's no one else within miles of this place."

I reminded him that this was to be an early-morning hunt and that I specifically did not want to be there in the evening. He angrily responded that Ed told him that he was not to leave before 8:30. WAIT A MINUTE . . . who the hell was the customer here? Tempers escalated, and it was obvious that this guide/hunter relationship was clearly damaged beyond repair. I told Charlie that I wanted to depart NOW! Charlie waved in the general direction of the horses and said they were over in that direction, and if I wanted to go, just go (some guide, huh).

I managed to find the horses just fine, without a guide, however the distance I traveled was great, the terrain incredibly difficult, and the pain shooting from my knees became absolutely unbearable. The rugged mountainside wore heavy on my injured knees. I truly needed a good night's rest. Charlie arrived at the horses from a different direction. It turned out Charlie took a much easier route back that crossed over a ridge just east of where we were glassing, and I assumed that he was not aware of this easy route before he sent me and my bad knees on the more difficult one (maybe yes and maybe no). I explained again to Charlie that things had to change. Not that anyone was right or wrong only that guide arrangements going forward had to be different, and we needed to meet with Ed on our return to base camp. Charlie wanted nothing to do with confronting Ed about a change. Unfortunately Ed was the person in charge of this guide set up, and I intended to tell him that a different guide arrangement had to be made. In truth, I was already prepared to do my own guide work.

On hearing this Charlie got very upset and said again that Ed told him to stay out and not to return until after dark. This kid had an unsettling fear for what Ed might say or do and there was a relationship problem between the two that was anything but transparent yet difficult for me to define. I told him that Ed had no room to talk because he returned to camp with the other guide and hunter the day before just when the rainstorm appeared. They hadn't stayed out until dark and made a run for camp as soon as the storm hit. Charlie was not aware of that but I could sense a deeper problem between these guys and wanted nothing to do with it, nor did I want to throw any fuel onto an existing dispute. I told Charlie I would tell Ed that, as the customer, I wanted to return before dark and Charlie had no choice but to return to base camp. This subcontracting guide service seemed to be experiencing an impossible time understanding the rudimentary basics of customer service.

My Plan

My knees continued to send me messages loud and clear that they were in need of rest and/or medical attention. Even with an extra dose of Aleve, my right knee continued to swell. Still I was positive that I could force one more climb up through the mountains and over to the spot were those bulls had been congregating. After that I would work the Wood River for the balance of my hunt.

The Wood River at this point ran west to east, located just to the northwest of the base camp. Reaching it was a very easy walk using my now hand-carved walking stick. Phase two of my plan, for the balance of the hunt, was to position myself a short distance upriver and downwind in the early morning. This morning approach would be completed no later than 6 a.m., not be departing camp at 8:30 a.m. as these high-priced and bacteria-tolerant guides seemed to prefer. The winds were strong each day, however they held a decided preference for 230 degrees on the compass rose. That southwest approach would work well with an upriver hunt along the Wood River. Going downstream in the event of a more northerly wind was doable but not my preference. If the winds persisted out of the north, I had already identified a mountainside that I previously glassed just southeast of the base camp that looked good to me and was a relatively easy climb. There was also a flat spot south of the mountain where I could set up to glass the area using my binoculars or spotting scope. I would just stuff my backpack with some food, spare clothes, water, and Aleve then sit back and take in the beauty of the marvelous mountains while I glassed for and hunted moose.

I had my plan to use if needed, and it would work just fine. I was also convinced that my plan would produce a moose. I would only need help with the dressing and packing out of the meat.

As an additional side note, four days later a moose was taken by a hunter from Wasilla, Alaska in the river area precisely where I had mentally set up this solo hunt.

RETURN TO BASE CAMP

On returning to base camp, ironically well after dark, I met Ed, and before I was able to make my formal guide-change request he launched into a description of the hunting plan he had for the next day. This plan involved setting up a spike camp for me a few miles south of base camp and a separate plan for the second hunter in camp (who had yet to see a moose) that would place him a few miles north of base camp. Ed further explained that this move was needed because we had to get deeper into the backcountry to begin our daily hunting activity. Other hunters had entered the surrounding Wood River area and they would complicate the prospects of finding a bull moose of legal size. He also told me that he would personally lead the way to select my spike camp location. Once selected, Ed would not stay there because he said he was having bear problems near one of his other camps that required his attention. Actually Ed was the person who, I think, was scheduled to be my guide, and he pawned me off on Charlie for no reason known to me. Charlie was not a licensed or registered hunting guide in Alaska. Absent cooking breakfast twice and loading up the mules on the second day, I honestly had no idea what Ed actually did throughout that hunt.

Now, I cannot say with any certainty but I was suspicious that Ed was doing some type of double dip. He should have been my guide for this week but may have been guiding a separate party at a different camp. Ed, as a subcontracted guide, may have received a payment from my outfitter to serve as my guide and then worked as a guide for a second party in an adjacent hunting area. Later, I would have more reason to believe that to be true.

This new plan of Ed's unfortunately did not separate Charlie and me, as Ed planned to depart with the horses and mules as soon as we located a spike camp site and unloaded the gear. While continuing with Charlie as a guide was not my wish, I recognized that there was a problem of some sort between Ed and Charlie and wanted no part of it, nor did I want to cause added grief for Charlie who I believed to be an individual incapable of handling any stress. I took Charlie aside and told him what Ed planned and if he wanted to give it a try I would support it and Charlie agreed. Charlie clearly disliked me but his intense fear of Ed overrode all else.

Hell, at this point I didn't trust any of these three characters and wanted to minimize my exposure to all three of them. I was in this great land to hunt a moose, and I could hunt alone just fine if needed.

Hunting Day Five

In the early morning (approximately 8:30 – that was early, I guess) we were saddled up and on our way. Three men on horses pulled one mule that carried the supplies we needed to set up this new spike camp. Ed lead the way to find the new campsite and he demonstrated that he was an outstanding horseman as he worked his way through the woods, mountains, creeks, and marshland. Unlike Charlie, Ed knew these woods very well. He also picked a spot on a flat area (opposed to Charlie's wishes) that was ideal for our needs. I wish things had been different on this hunt and Ed would have served as my guide. Ed clearly knew what he was doing when it came to hunting moose, he knew this area well, and more important did a much better job of listening when I asked questions about our direction and navigation through the dense forest.

I still had plenty of knicker treats for my horse and blessed every step it took.

Before Ed departed with the horses and pack mule he explained to me that he would be back the next day then changed that to two days. He then held up two fingers and said two days again, thought for a moment and held up a third finger and said empathically "Two days, but no more than three." I would never see Ed again! I continued to suspect that Ed had arranged a second hunting party business and was standing in front of me on that mountainside mentally trying to juggle his time schedule.

After dismounting and unloading our gear I started with the tent setup, and Charlie asked if I would glass an area for moose that was just south of our position. He wanted to set the camp up alone, and if I checked this area for moose, we could then climb the mountains to the west to get to the ridge overlooking the valley where we saw the six bulls two days earlier.

Fine by me as I'd much rather hunt than pitch a tent. Setting up camp was Charlie's job anyway. Also I was able to identify a mountainside on this brief solo hunt that I thought looked very promising for moose maybe later in the week. This is the mountain that would compensate for a steady wind from the north, and today it was clearly out of the southwest. Interesting too after approximately two hours passed, Charlie came to where I was glassing and advised that the spike camp was set up, and we could start our climb to the west.

Now viewing this spike camp Charlie had set up was certainly interesting. Sigmund Freud would have had a field day analyzing this antisocial layout. The two-man tent was set up for my use and was separate from the actual camp area. About ten yards away under a conifer tree, facing away from my tent, Charlie had his personal camp set up with a nice rock fire pit in front of it all arranged in a way not to be shared with anyone using the two man tent. It was like two separate camps in one. Pretty clear message. Charlie didn't want any part of me, and I genuinely wished that Ed would have dropped me off to hunt alone, leaving my immature guide back at base camp.

It would be ever so difficult to make the most out of this state of affairs, but I would endeavor to do my best. Like Orion, I was here to hunt moose not serve as a psychoanalyst.

Reaching the glassing ridge was difficult but much easier using Charlie's (new found) ridge route. The first leg required climbing over a mountain that exceeded 4,000 feet, following its ridge line, and proceeding on to the ridge where we were glassing at 3,400 feet. On examining the topographical maps of the area before departing home I did not believe that I would be above the 2,000 foot level or at most the 2,500 foot level on this hunt, and the extra 1,600 foot climb was anything but easy. Once on the ridge I found winds at this altitude to be much more pronounced, making travel even more difficult. Climbing into this wind was like riding a motorcycle at full throttle without a helmet or wind screen for protection.

We took up positions on the ridge about thirty yards apart and glassed this valley until nearly dark without luck, and then Charlie spotted a bull off to our left. His eyes were good, and it took me a few minutes even with my twelve power binoculars to locate the moose. I later checked with my GPS, and the moose was precisely 1.2 miles away from our ridge. Now that was 1.2 miles in a direct line, a distance that crossed over two mountainsides with thick alders. Reaching that moose would prove to be very demanding following the terrain (not straight line), and here too every step on that soft, spongy ground would be difficult.

We both debated the possibility of a final stalk on this bull. The distance was great, and for a significant time on our final stalk we would be in the open and clearly visible to the bull. The good news was that the wind was directly in my favor, unfortunately it was also ripping through the valley at about sixty knots. The wind was so strong that it made it impossible to hold the binoculars or spotting scope steady enough to determine the size of the bull's antlers. Charlie believed that it was a big and legal bull. The antlers looked to be somewhere near the fifty-inch mark (ADF&G regulation), but that was difficult to determine at this distance. (Man, where was that long distance tape measure when you needed it?) We had to determine that the bull also carried four brow tines to make it a legal bull, and we could not make that determination at this distance combating such a strong wind.

I desperately searched the valley below with my binoculars hoping to find another bull near enough to identify as legal and closer to this spotting perch. I wanted to find one nearby that would allow me to complete the final stalk without ending up in the hospital. This bull to the left presented an unyielding challenge.

No closer bulls were at hand, and my choice was to go after the 1.2-mile monster. It would be a physically demanding final stalk with two good knees, and this bull might bolt before we closed in for a shot. Here Charlie did prove to be a very good hunter, leading the way on our long stalk. Several times when we were in the open the bull turned his head in our direction using his big white palmed antlers to assist his already excellent hearing in trying to determine what it was that was moving in his direction. At this time the near gale force winds aided immensely in masking our identity.

It is difficult to describe the adrenalin rush present on this final stalk. I was soaked with sweat and my brain became numb to the pain from my knees. We finally reached a wooded area lying between the bull and us. Then as we reached the far side of that area, nearer the bull it was clear that we could go no further without spooking this giant bull as he was now on full alert. The window of opportunity for a shot was there but only open for a moment or two. This shot would be a long one for my 30-06 as it was more than three hundred yards and all the time spent on the rifle range had to pay dividends. The bull was a monster, and I remember thinking *"Hey, maybe those Chinese guys were wrong, I do need a cannon."*

I placed a round in the chamber, turned off the safety, got into my shooting position, raised my rifle, and damn, the heavy sweat and perspiration caused my glasses to completely fog over as soon as I brought the rifle into shooting position. This happened two more times before I was able to get the sight picture that I needed. I refused to shoot until I was absolutely certain that I was on the mark. The long distance between the bull and me, coupled with the light caliber of this ammunition demanded that my shooting be excellent. My first shot was perfectly placed.

Author with giant bull moose taken at over 300 yards

I sat in place for a moment, physically beaten, soaked in sweat, both knees swollen and painful, but I had successfully completed my hunt and Orion would have certainly approved!

It was now getting dark, and we were a long way from spike camp. A tremendous amount of work remained to be done to dress out this moose and properly prepare and wrap the meat for temporary storage in the woods. We were literally miles from the spike camp and needed to make a plan of action.

We had two options. One was to stay with the moose all night and sleep in the open. The second was return to spike camp for the night and return in the morning. We decided that with darkness near at hand it might be best to return to camp and then finish dressing the moose in the morning. I told Charlie that it was not likely that I would be able to make the trip over to the moose from spike camp in the morning as my injured knees simply needed rest. He said that it was no problem and correctly added that dressing the moose was his job.

The return to base camp was a long walk and a killer for my knees, but the thrill of the successful hunt made the walking much easier. I was right when putting together my final hunting plan and deciding that one trip over the mountains was all I would be able to muster. My goal was accomplished, and there would be no need to hunt the river basin going forward.

Sleep came easy this night, and it was the most restful night I had since my arrival in the last frontier.

CHAPTER 12

CONCLUSION OF THE HUNT
(GUIDE EVALUATION)

On hunting day five, Charlie and I split up. He had the most difficult task on this date and suggested that I stay in camp until Ed showed up with the horses and mules. Little did I know at that time, Ed never intended to return. From where the moose was located Charlie would have an easier and shorter route back to base camp by following the Wood River versus a return to this spike camp first, and I suggested that he take that route. On this morning I felt that I could make the trip back to base camp on my own. My knees were feeling better after a good night's rest, plus I was familiar with the area, woods, streams, and swamps and could easily navigate the most direct route to base camp using my GPS and compass (Lewis and Clark should have had one of these GPS units).

We each loaded up our backpacks and set off in different directions, I would see very little of Charlie for the remainder of my time at the Wood River base camp.

My travel did not cover much ground before those familiar messages started to travel from my knees to my brain. The pain got much worse as I moved through the woods and I mentally debated turning back, but I wanted nothing to do with that spike camp, and besides my goal was set, I was determined to get through. When I eventually stopped for a rest break, a look at my GPS proved to be a little depressing as it indicated over three miles to go (in a direct line of sight). It would be a long and painful trek, through the thick boreal forest back to base camp. A long hike indeed, but I made it.

Pack animals off to somewhere --- I do not know

Back at base camp things were quiet . . . too quiet. The horses and mules were gone, and the camp was empty. Now with all the horses and mules gone it appeared to me that something was amiss. This subcontracting guide service had to be up to something. There were three people, two of whom were registered guides whose job and sole responsibility was to take care of two hunters, and yet one hunter (me) got relegated to a non-guide hunt while the two guides headed off in another direction with one hunter and all the animals. There wasn't any possible way to retrieve my moose meat from the woods with all the animals gone. Ed had to be pulling a double-dip on my outfitter who was paying for two guides and twelve animals to provide guide support. His wife worked very hard to assure that all the camp food and feed for the animals got air shipped to base camp on time. Nevertheless, there were no animals present, and I had no guide. Yes, it was quiet, too quiet.

It was Wednesday, and I remained confident that I would be able to get word back to the outfitter that I needed to be picked up. My hunt was over both physically and mentally. I wanted to depart. My cell phone, unfortunately, did not work even at 4,000 feet, but I was sure the pilot would be making supply drop-off flights, or I might be able to get word to him through another pilot who might land at the airstrip near camp.

No luck. Poor weather conditions at the departure point continued to ground my pilot and his Piper Cub.

Another very real concern I had was the recovery and care of the meat left in the field. Recovery of the meat was very important to me and yet this guide service made no arrangements to have pack animals available to do the job. Air temperatures also became a problem because the days remained unseasonably warm and the meat would spoil or be taken by bears or wolves if left uncared for in the field. Had Ed, the leader, simply assumed I would not get a moose? Ed never returned to camp while I was there. Perhaps he thought that he could wait for my departure to avoid the burden of answering the many questions he knew I had. Why did you not return as you said? Why did you take all the pack animals? Why was I given so little assistance with this hunt?

In Ed's eyes it was probably not likely that our paths would ever cross again, so what the heck, who cares?

While my focus on this hunting day six was to depart base camp and conclude my hunt, it was not to be as the adverse weather conditions coupled with poor communications resulted in an additional four-day delay. This extended delay did yield some positive experiences. New hunters were coming in for the third week of hunting season, and they were being flown into this particular site as it was the best area to construct rafts for float hunting down the Wood River. The Wood River widened out at this point, running away from the airstrip and was generally deep enough to support rafts. Floatation support on the river this year was poor as the summer had been very dry. Other hunters told me that the river farther down was so low that rafters would be spending huge amounts of time unloading their rafts to reduce weight. They would be forced to drag their rafts over shallow sections of the river and then reload the rafts where the river deepened. Tons of unanticipated work awaited every rafting party, and new hunters were flying in from Fairbanks almost everyday. Also, the airplanes used by the rafters were much bigger than the Cub I came in on and could handle more turbulent air. In addition, the air route from Fairbanks did not share the poor weather and high wind phenomena that my pilot had to face. Two of these pilots were able to convey a message on my behalf to my pilot but their efforts were to no avail.

The river rafts being dropped off were large, unassembled for air transportation, and came in two basic forms. One form was a standard type inflatable variety, and the other was more of a twin pontoon raft with a frame that required a considerable amount of time to assemble. It was fun meeting these new hunters, helping to unload the big Cessna 206s and 207s, and prepare the river rafts. One Cessna 207 carried a load that was just a mite too tail heavy for me, but the weight distribution didn't seem to bother the pilot. A tail heavy airplane could be difficult to handle if you lost power because a pilot needed to get the airplanes nose down to secure air speed. Tail heavy airplanes were problems too if the aircraft got caught in a spin -- not much hope getting out of the spin, and the plane would "pancake" in at a high rate of speed.

There was an interesting group of six hunters who arrived from Fairbanks on Friday. This collection of dandies required five round trips in a Cessna 207 to transport all their food and camping gear. These guys assembled three large rafts with one raft set up to be used solely as a beer raft. I counted over sixteen cases of beer on that third raft! They were a jolly crew who had a grand time organizing their equipment and launching their rafts. When they finally got underway I could still hear them singing and laughing as they rounded the first bend a quarter mile down river.

The last frontier of the last frontier was starting to change!

Just a "tad" tail heavy

Standard raft ready for launch

Cata-rafts under construction on the Wood River

I met a new hunter who was hunting solo and using a canoe-shaped single-man raft to travel through the Wood River drainage. I admired people like him as it took courage to face the dangers and rigors of river travel running solo -- anything could happen and no one could be there to help. He did have a rented satellite telephone with him to use for any extreme emergency as well as contacting his wife at the end of each day (next time out I will also rent or buy one of these potentially lifesaving devises). He was kind enough to let me use his telephone to get word to my outfitter to pick me up. The winds and flight conditions at my outfitter's departure point continued to be bad and my pickup was not scheduled until Saturday at 2:00 p.m. Saturday passed with no pickup.

These last days in camp were spent alone as Charlie was spending most of his time at the guide's primary base camp somewhere to the northeast (I believe I drove him away with my constant questions about retrieving my moose meat). His absence was no problem for me as I had a book to read and the periodic company of other hunters. I also enjoyed cooking so after I returned to base camp, I set out searching for the food catch. Here I located a food bonanza. What I found under the main tent area, secured in large plastic containers held down by large rocks was the "mother load" of camp food. There was thick-sliced bacon, eggs, sausage, caribou sausage, coffee, and bread for breakfast. One of the guides had told me earlier that the outfitter's wife did not send out bread, but here I found one plastic container full of bread. I couldn't imagine why anyone would want to store (and not use) so many loaves of bread. I found steaks sealed in plastic, canned food, prepared meals, lunch meats, cheese, mandarin oranges, apples, and fruit juices but no crab legs! Even without the king crab this large food catch was still the "Holy Grail" of camp food.

Now, as the customer, I helped myself to the food catch and set about cooking. Most cooking had to be engineered on an open fire to save that old and failing Coleman stove for breakfast preparations, but that was no problem. Crippled knees did not slow me down here, and with every meal I served myself generous portions. It was fun and my only concern was that my cooking certainly sent out tantalizing odors throughout the woods -- to bears and wolves. You can bet that my trusty 30-06 was at the ready.

I was surprised on Saturday late afternoon to see the guide, Joe, and his hunter return, but no Ed. The other hunter had not been successful on his hunt despite having the services of both camp guides plus all the camp horses and mules. I know he was disappointed as he had hunted hard all week yet went home empty.

Sunday morning my pilot was able to fly his Piper Super Cub into base camp. I had my gear all packed and ready to go, and he appreciated my preparation as he was behind schedule due to the adverse weather. He loaded my gear into the plane, I immediately climbed into the Piper, with rifle and walking stick in hand, and we were on our way. The ride back over the mountains was smooth, and from this perch in the sky we saw numerous game animals below. We flew directly over a giant bull moose and cow at low altitude and the bull was shaking his antlers in a frenzy throwing his head from side to side in a warning to us to stay away. The sight of this bull threatening us was dramatic and comical as he was prepared to defend his ground, protect his cow, and was sending a warning to the airplane flying above to beware. My flight this day was pure enjoyment, and Lance once again took time to share some interesting flying stories with me   He was a great aviation guide. This was the final day of my hunt, and it was a great day. Tonight would be shower time and a hot restaurant meal. Life was good.

Charlie and Joe were both in camp at the time I departed however I cannot remember either of them saying good-bye, but heck, they didn't say hello, so there certainly was no reason to say good-bye.

I believe that working as a guide required more than Charlie was willing or able to provide. He was an experienced hunter, but I think he lacked the temperament or interpersonal skills needed to become a reliable big game guide. Clearly, Charlie was not skilled when it came to people management!

In life and in business we are all called on to be people managers, sometimes we respond, doing well at it. And sometimes we do not. We too receive opportunities to serve as guides. Sometimes we pass, and sometimes we fail.

CHAPTER 13

REFLECTIONS ON THE HUNT
(OUTFITTER BUSINESS EVALUATION)

My hunting experience was not what I anticipated but was a hunting learning experience for sure. The hunting outfitter/guide arrangement was a monumental failure, but it too was a learning experience.

Translating this experience into a business setting, to allow an examination of what went wrong, it is clear that the people management side of the ledger did not go well. It was not just the bad people management between Charlie, Ed, and me, which I (personally) was unable to manage. Poor people management skills came to play throughout the entire subcontracting debacle and those unfortunate circumstances need not have happened.

Upon personal examination of what could have been done differently, to make things better, it's obvious that work performance follow-up was needed. In any business endeavor a performance plan is required that establishes measurable goals. Competent business managers set goals, target performance standards and measure results. Once a decision is made to subcontract work, or send your (customer) responsibilities outside, engagement in some type of monitoring process is a must. In chapter fifteen I will give you examples of some HR work that I contracted out. One was the total bundling up of 401k services with an outside service company, and the second was direct involvement of an outside service company for group insurance products. In each situation the work done outside the company was excellent and, honestly, completed far better than I could have ever managed in-house, but it was not a "contract-out-and-walk-away" situation. I made time to meet with those providers on a regular basis, and designed a process to measure the results of service performance through statistical process control (SPC). I knew, through diligent follow up and customized SPC validation processes, that my company (their customer) received a very good return on investment.

There were times throughout my time in the woods where the outfitter could have checked on activities of his subcontractor. His pilot was in the area servicing other clients and could have taken time to land and ask. I saw him fly over a few times after that first day and wished that he would have landed so I could get word back to the outfitter (who was hunting with a separate client only twelve miles distant) that I needed a guide change or hunt termination. Other communication arrangements could have been made by the outfitter to personally stop by, or have a trusted aide stop by, to assure that the subcontract arrangements were being completed to the customer's satisfaction. Costly yes, but the fee for this hunt was expensive as well. In addition, while cell phones proved to be worthless in this steep, secluded mountainous terrain, other seasoned hunters brought satellite phones that operated reasonably well. They were available on a rental basis and not that expensive.

One hunter I met from Wasilla, Alaska, told me a story of how a friend of his credits his rented satellite phone for saving his life. Each call from the rented phone was only $1.75 and, in this case, a lifesaver. On my next journey into this type of terrain you can bet that I will definitely posses a satellite telephone. An additional communications tool might be a CB-type radio arrangement. Here antennas would be needed and strategically placed, but that could be done - also at a low cost.

People problems can be fixed. In this situation the repair job could have easily been managed by the "C" word -- communications.

I must submit that the "C" word is one of those words easy to say but not always easy to practice. A "real-life" example of failed communications was my interface/altercation with Charlie. The "C" word is not so easy to employ. I worked with a guy a few years back who told me when he graduated from college a professor advised him, as he was about to begin his business career, the biggest problem he would face in business was communications - communications, communications, communications. He further advised him that when he would end his career and retire, the biggest problem facing business at that time would be communications - communications, communications, communications. I think that professor was on to something.

Past performance of a subcontractor is a very good indicator of future performance, but it is not a given. In this situation the subcontractor performance in the prior season was reported by the outfitter as being good. Regardless, I suspect that the hunting party departing at the time I arrived may have given the outfitter information, upon return, that might have/should have raised his concern. Ultimately, with customer in mind, the outfitter cannot escape the validation responsibility. Fault here is inescapable viewing circumstances from a business standpoint. The outfitter failed as a hunter (poor sub-contracting) and he failed as a guide (no follow-up).

Remember this lesson. When contracting out any business service accept responsibility for performance validation. The integrity of the process rests in your hands, no others.

CHAPTER 14

END OF THE JOURNEY
(MORE COMMENTS ON
EMPLOYEE COMMUNICATIONS)

Sad to say that on returning from my hunt in the last frontier, I only felt a tremendous sense of relief that the hunt segment of my journey was finally over. In too many ways it was a torturous ordeal. Here was the hunt that I had dreamed of as a kid, planned to take as a young army soldier, and spent the last ten months engaged in almost daily preparation for, and now all I felt was relief that it was over. The next day, when my pilot flew back with the moose meat from my hunt it only added to my disappointment as much of the meat had spoiled. The meat was spoiled, in part, because it sat too long in the woods waiting to be picked up by the guides with their mules – those mules that mysteriously disappeared from base camp to do something, somewhere, I do not know. A portion of the meat had apparently not been properly wrapped by Charlie when field dressing the bull in the woods, coupled with unseasonably warm weather only accelerated the spoiling process.

My head was filled with so many questions: How could this hunt possibly have unfolded as it did? At age sixty-one did my brain fail to comprehend the realities of a danger-riddled hunt deep into the last frontier? Did I set my expectations too high? Was I an inadequate hunter who had no business embarking on this hunting adventure in the first place? Lastly, why even though I was successful in procuring a bull moose did I feel so dejected?

My enthusiasm for the hunt could not have been greater, my preparation could not have been more complete, and yet my expectations for the moose hunting episode of this journey clearly exceeded results. Once in a letter to his brother, Theo, artist Vincent VanGogh wrote: "You should never trust the situation when you are without difficulty." My un-guided hunt scenario did not lack difficulty, it was a daunting task and could only be viewed with trust in VanGogh's troubled mind.

As a learning experience this hunting part of my journey could have provided much more, but it did not. As a hunter I could have learned much more, but I did not. This hunt could have provided outdoor camaraderie, but it did not . . . such a sad ending to a long-awaited experience.

Back from the hunt I met with the outfitter company owner, and related my unpleasant hunting experience, including my dissatisfaction with the guide support service received. He empathized with me, sharing my disappointment, and his wife, the administrative leader of the business, went to lengths making things right with me regarding the spoiled meat.

My evaluation of this outfitter (business owner) remains potentially positive as I have been told he is a good big-game hunter who wanted to build a reputable outfitting business. As a guide (absent his subcontracting debacle with Ed, Joe and Charlie) he might also rank in that twenty-five percent referenced earlier. Therefore, if he is a hunter and a guide, some leadership potential may be present to engineer a business enterprise.

The hunting/guide job match between Charlie and I was a failure from the start, and while the outfitter held primary responsibility (he was the recruiter), I must accept some of the blame. You see, HR people need to excel in job/worker match activity (hunting), and here I did not do a thorough job. Jim Rimmel would advise that I didn't go that extra mile and paid a price. My job, even as the customer, was to find out in advance specifically who my guide would be and take time to verify his credentials (easy to do online). I also recognize that in the employment job/match process nothing, I emphasize nothing, is a better indicator of work performance than good work reference checks. Time taken to call past clients of the guide (successful and unsuccessful hunters) to learn more about the guide, what did he know, what could he do, would have been time well spent (part of planning). No Jim, I did not go that extra mile and I paid a price.

I did gain personally in many ways. I underwent a very unique learning experience, was successful in my hunt, and for a few days was actually part of that last frontier of the last frontier. I didn't just see it, I lived it. I saw the greatness of the land, took deep breaths of clear mountain air, drank water from beautiful mountain streams, endured wilderness hardships, and could feel, smell and taste the wind, rain, and sun in the last frontier. It was great!

You might ask if I would do it again, and I can say most certainly yes although there would be changes. My preparation would be even more complete thanks to this very demanding learning experience. I might also need to take my knee braces and walking stick along with some renewed determination, but I would do it in a heart beat. The land I hunted in was magnificent, there is no other place like it on earth. I can still feel it. I can still taste it. I can still smell it. Bad guides and exploding volcanoes aside, the great land of Alaska will always hold a powerful magnetic draw. In this verse from Robert Service's poem "Spell of the Yukon" he says it best about the great land up north:

> *"There's a land where the mountains are nameless,*
> *And the rivers all run God knows where;*
> *There are lives that are erring and aimless,*
> *And deaths that just hang by a hair;*
> *There are hardships that nobody reckons;*
> *There are valleys unpeopled and still;*
> *There's a land-oh, it beckons and beckons,*
> *And I want to go back – and I will"*

DRIVE HOME

My return trip home was much more direct. The drive through Alaska, Yukon, and British Columbia was one I looked forward to but still moved through this marvelous country with objectivity. The hunt was over and I was on a mission to get home.

It was first to Whitehorse from Fairbanks where I stopped at a convenient hotel on the main highway leading into Whitehorse. At the beginning of this book I said it would be a book about people management or "miss-management" and with that in mind I need to comment on an employee communication sign I saw at this hotel in Whitehorse. The hotel was constructed to have the appearance of a European Chalet. It sat directly across the road from the city airport and was appropriately called the Airport Chalet. The hotel was comfortable, the people working there friendly, and the food was good. Eating dinner that evening I happened to notice a sign approximately sixteen inches square that was nailed to the dinning room wall near the kitchen entrance that read in bold face print:

"If you have time to lean,
You have time to clean!"

Please, any manager reading this book, give some serious thought to what this sign really said. Clearly, it was intended to be a clever message from hotel management to employees, admonishing them not to be lazy and to get back to work. Possibly, some employees had been seen standing around not busy when there was cleaning work to be done, so the manager took action by placing this sign on the wall. Now, what this sign really said was that management knew their employees were lazy goof-offs (an indictment if you will) and therefore directed them back to work.

Were there actually managers out there, so naive to think that a single employee of this organization would read the sign and really give a crap? The sign was at best a joke with the workers, and most likely offensive to employees who were not lazy goof-offs, standing around when there was cleaning to be done (which might just happen to be ninety-eight percent of the hotel workforce). This sign also branded the restaurant employees as lazy to every single customer sitting in the dining room, because management elected to post this beauty where all the restaurant customers could see it. It would have been better (but not much) if management would have placed this notice in the kitchen area or any work area not open to the public. Too often managers take action against many for the acts of a few. Signs such as these are productively destructive and certainly do not serve any motivational value.

I urge managers reading this book to give this thought because I see these signs and this negative management message in nearly every business establishment I enter. Trust me; there is more than a fair-chance that you have some hanging on walls or bulletin boards where you work. They are the not-so-clever signs we managers put up with little thought given to how they will be received by employees or customers.

Interestingly, signs like this one also serve as ammunition for Dilbert-type cartoons. I had the opportunity years ago to attend a meeting where Scott Adams (Dilbert creator) made a speech to our group and his speech was fantastic. In that speech he said that much of his cartoon material was sent to him by e-mail from people in the workplace who wanted to share with him the stupid yet real things managers had said or done in their organization. Scott took note of the real work-world event and then turned it into a Dilbert Cartoon that people would read and laugh – the serious truth can be funny. Here, I guess Scott could draw the pointy hair boss nailing this sign on a cubicle wall with Wally, Dilbert, and Alice watching him, in disbelief, while they stand leaning at about a sixty degree angle.

People management is not easy. Douglas McGregor was a behavioral scientist, one of my favorites, who authored a number of books on leadership and motivation and is probably best known for his writing on Theory X and Theory Y management styles. McGregor was literally decades ahead of his time and his genius has proven to be timeless. His X & Y philosophy is much deeper than most realize as it goes beyond simply identifying a style of management as being rigid, untrusting or not. What resides at the heart of McGregor's philosophy has to do with the assumptions managers make about people. In short, the assumptions managers make about people (good and bad) will very often result in a mirror-like performance. If managers assume a person is lazy and will "lean instead of clean," there is a good chance that the person will respond in kind. If managers assume that a person working for them cannot be trusted there is no reason, no motivation, for that person to act in any different way. Making assumptions, such as this one, only serve as negative feedback to the individual. As with the Pygmalion affect, this negative conditioning, once in place, can be difficult or impossible to turn around.

Along this line let me tell you that years ago, I met a general manager of a manufacturing shop that employed around four hundred people. This general manager had a refreshing philosophy regarding people at work. He said that people are intrinsically honest. They do not steal, and when they come to work, they arrive at the work site wanting to do a good job. (Yeah for management!) Employee theft at this manufacturing plant was not measurable because it did not exist. Now, this was a plant engaged in building large machinery, with skilled trades and assembly people working a three-shift operation. They had no fence around the building, no security guards at the doors, no security cameras watching workers, and comparatively few supervisors overseeing the work being done. They did however have good inventory controls on tools, parts, and equipment and were aware that things in the shop simply did not walk away.

The general manager told all his employees that if they had a personal need for anything that might be company property to just let a supervisor know what they needed and why. As example, skilled trades workers would often ask for bolts, nuts, or fasteners for home projects, and the company would record what items were requested (for inventory) and would always honor any reasonable request made. Also, workers, on occasion, would want to borrow tools such as drills, sanders, or other machine tools, and the company would let them sign out and take home any tools not immediately needed for production. You see the general manager assumed that his workers were intrinsically honest and placed trust in them. The workers in turn respected and appreciated this trust placed in them, and consequently no worker abused the privileges they were provided. Workers simply did not steal from this company that trusted them and paid their wages. In Chapter 15 I will provide an opposite example (Company Z) that produced disastrous results.

When managers see "don't lean" signs on the walls in their business, it's best to take them down. Clever as they may be written, they do more harm than good.

Well, I was certainly not leaning or cleaning on this day and got back on the road early, headed for home. I skipped Watson Lake and drove on to Fort Nelson, then on to Edmonton, and there were no two-night stays along the route. All my driving through Canada was easy as the roads were clear, the highways were well maintained, plus the scenery and wildlife were true wonders to behold. I had my binoculars handy and took time to stop to watch the large game animals along the way. Once, in northern British Columbia, I stopped to view the biggest black bear I had ever seen – a true monster. He was an awesome beast, and it was apparent that he knew it as his movements were deliberate. He displayed no fear and walked slowly with the confidence of an apex predator through the lightly forested mountainside adjacent to the highway. He was no more than thirty yards away at one point, and as I trained my twelve power binoculars on him, the bear seemed to be standing next to me. I could detail every feature of his face with those deep dark menacing eyes staring right back. Be assured that the only thing next to me was my car, with the door open, and the distance between me and that open door was, maybe, a millimeter!

After a courteous but time-consuming stop at U.S. Customs it was on to Minot, North Dakota (no speed traps this time), and Wisconsin where I opted to skip "The Dells" even though the tourist season was over, and I would assume room rates were no longer quadrupled. I left Wisconsin in the early morning for my final drive to Ohio and home. Here the only bad road traveled n this journey (and it was a horrible nightmare) was route 294 going around Chicago. What a monumental mess. I passed four cars parked at the side of this road with blown out tires, two of them had both tires on the right side of their car blown out caused by the rough road surface. This road provided a lot of driving grief and proved to be a financial nightmare for many on that day. Yes, route 294 around Chicago was the most dangerous and treacherous stretch of road I faced on this entire trip. It actually took on the appearance of the Alcan highway when it was under construction during WWII.

Why is it that large construction projects in every big city sooner or later take on a look similar to that of the "Big Dig" construction project in Boston? Major projects in large cities tend to be plagued by gigantic cost overruns, construction delays that exceed reason, and miles of road torn up with stretches of the road designated by large signs as being work zones where you never see any work being done. Crazy, but the only smooth parts of this road around Chicago were the off-ramp detours leading up to the numerous toll booths the city employed to stop all traffic and hijack enormous sums of money. Mysteriously this money, once collected, must vanish into thin air as finished and smooth highways around Chicago never seem to materialize.

I covered 3,904 miles in six days or 651 driving miles were averaged per day returning home with no speed tickets (I didn't speed), and absent the highway around Chicago it was a truly enjoyable driving experience.

When arriving home my car's trip odometer read 9,494.8 miles. The travel to Fairbanks (with side trips) was 4,163 miles, topped off with

1,427.8 miles driven in Alaska and the more direct route of 3,904 miles for the return home. My travel included city driving, construction/traffic tie-ups, as well as some Alaska off-road hill climbing that resulted in the use of 317.475 gallons of gas. That equates to 29.907 aggregate miles per gallon for the entire journey (Not too bad for a heavily loaded four door Avalon sedan, with a V-6 engine). U.S. gas prices escalated (nearly doubled) in a short period prior to my journey and yet the average price for a gallon of gas in the U.S. remained thirty-six percent below the average price in Canada (Fuel consumption in Canada was converted to U.S. gallons and U.S. dollars for comparison).

Was it worth it? Yes indeed it was. What a tremendous learning experience. This unbelievable journey more than fulfilled my transitional desires. I did see and was able to experience things that are often only dreamed of, and the geography of the land was spectacular. It was the adventure of a lifetime that included thrills and hardships exceeding my imagination. I hunted more than just a moose on this transitional journey and the hunting was fruitful in nearly every way.

THE SPIRIT OF ORION

Readers must always remember that there is the spirit of Orion in each and every one of us. We humans hunt throughout our lives, and we hunt in our own world, our own living environment very well. We were biologically and mechanically engineered to hunt, and we go about our hunting almost automatically each and every day. We hunt for the basics of food and shelter, for the best deals on home appliances, the automobile that best fits our needs, the clothes we wear, the best parking spot, the best family doctor, the best hospitals, the solutions to work issues, and those positive interpersonal relationships. By our very nature we hunt in every activity we engage in, business management included. You do not need to be a big game hunter charging through the boreal forests with rifle in hand to embrace the spirit of Orion, we all have it, and we use those hunting skills naturally well.

Let me now "switch-gears" and, in addendum, focus on the HR Discipline to provide my thoughts on various components of HR Practice.

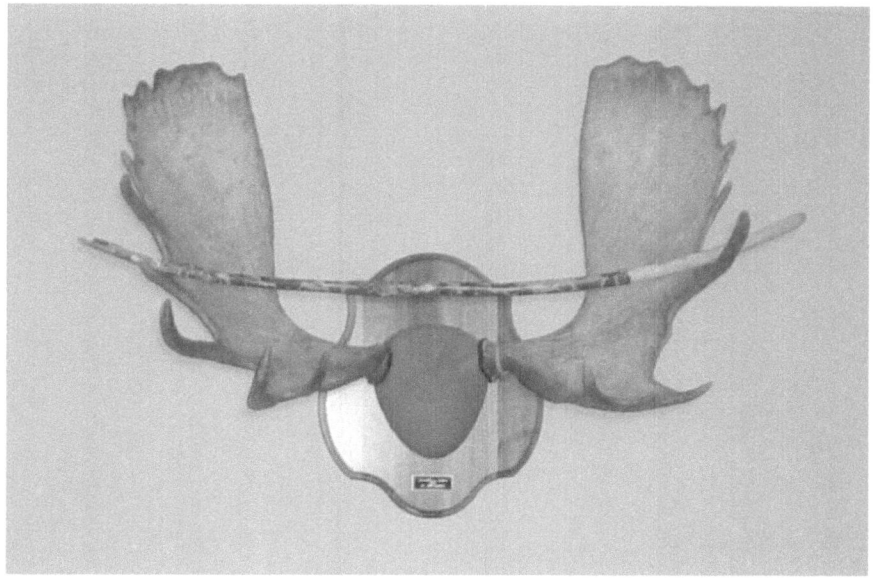

Trophy walking stick with moose rack

Principles of sound HR Management

CHAPTER 15

RULES AND IDEAS FOR THE PEOPLE MANAGEMENT BUSINESS

THREE KEY RULES:

Rule Number One: Know the business that your company is in, be it products or services and the cost of doing business. Know your competition. Know how your products or services are made, and most of all know your customers, and how they use your products or services. Think positive, measure your performance and be part of the team that gets things done.

Rule Number Two: Know the business that your company is in, be it products or services and the cost of doing business. Know your competition. Know how your products or services are made, and most of all know your customers, and how they use your products or services. Think positive, measure your performance and be part of the team that gets things done.

Rule Number Three: Know the business that your company is in, be it products or services and the cost of doing business. Know your competition. Know how your products or services are made, and most of all know your customers, and how they use your products or services. Think positive, measure your performance and be part of the team that gets things done.

You may think that for an HR person my rules are too focused on business costs and business numbers with too little focus on people working in the organization or, should I say, the "touchy-feely" component of work, but that's incorrect. In the human resource (aka personnel management) arena the business is numbers - very large numbers. I must add that if those numbers do not responsibly match your business requirements, then the need for any working people in your organization will soon disappear. You must always remember your businesses customers, and remember customer dollars pay all the bills; customers, customers, customers!

At my last job I had a boss named Joe Huss, and Joe was very good at understanding our business, recognizing customer needs, and he had an uncanny knack for comprehending numbers. Anytime I approached Joe with a new HR idea, new HR regulation, or newly concocted governmental obligation, I went prepared to answer his questions. They invariably were: How does this thing help our business support the customer? What is the cost of this thing? And what is the price if we just don't do it? (A very important question.)

These three straightforward questions focus directly on customer value and financial worth. Think about them for a few moments, and reflect on their business importance. Also, if you are a business leader, try asking the same questions in your business operation. At the least, you will generate some interest in rules one, two, and three.

For you human resource type folks, once you have mastered rules number One, Two and Three, you will be ready to launch into some of these additional ideas on general Human Resource/Personnel activities.

HR Ideas

Employment and Staffing

This is <u>the</u> basic people-manager responsibility and one that is never done to the 100 percent satisfaction of everyone involved. The key to doing the best job is to get the management team responsively engaged in the process from start to finish.

On hiring new employees, let me give you a real-world example of how not to do it that should be obvious to any business executive possessing even a miniscule amount of financial savvy. I was a personnel manager in the early 1970s (we didn't have HR back then) at a unionized manufacturing plant of about 740 workers. We were expanding our manufacturing and needed to add twenty-five new production workers, modify some existing equipment, and buy a new cut-off saw that, at the time, was priced at slightly over $10,000. Before we purchased that cut-off saw asset, we had to have our engineering department complete a feasibility study, sales had to provide customer use data, accounting had to calculate the payback and depreciation, purchasing had to secure competitive bids from several different suppliers, and finally, a team of talented engineers and manufacturing people had to visit each saw manufacturing site to evaluate the various cut-off saws before we made the decision to buy. This involved an immense amount of work and was very time consuming for our high priced executive staff, but we wanted to select the right saw for this important expansion project.

On the human acquisition side of this expansion equation, what do you think took place? The personnel manager (me) started recruiting those new twenty-five workers, and because this project was so important, I asked that members of the manufacturing team also to participate in the job candidate interviews and selections. They promptly declined and, in a way, complimented me by saying that it was my job - they were comfortable with me doing it just as had been done in the past.

Now with new workers being hired, think about these two things: first, human assets are unique as they are the only assets within your organization that can appreciate in value or deprecate in value, and it is here where the right job/worker match yields positive results. Conversely a physical asset like the cut-off saw depreciates in value from the very first day it's purchased --- the value goes down, never up. Second, take a minute to think about the cost implications. That cut-off saw was a $10,000 capital expenditure however hiring twenty-five new workers was exponentially more. Our plant hourly wage at that time ran around eleven dollars per hour, and our benefits "roll-up" cost added another forty-two percent. That equaled an annual cost of $32,490 per hire or $812,240 a year for all twenty-five new employees. More importantly it represented a financial cost that only increased. As an asset, humans can depreciate or appreciate in value but the cost of that asset only goes one way: up!

Give this example just a millisecond of thought, and tell me if it makes any sense. An entire team of talented managers, engineers, purchasing representatives, and manufacturing people worked on a $10,000 business expense, and yet one person was entrusted to make all the decisions regarding a business expense that was near $1,000,000 . . . Hello, anybody home?

Get management involvement in the entire planning and execution process when you start spending money on human assets.

Study your employment recruiting area, and know your sources well. Develop strong interview skills, build on those skills, and recognize that interviewing is an ever changing process. Few people possess good interview skills, and in my career, although I've met literally thousands of job interviewers, I seriously doubt that more than a mere handful are ones who I would describe as good interviewers.

In an employment interview, the interviewer must first put the candidate at ease, and then with the initial interview, there is generally only a short time available to secure the information you need to evaluate the candidate's match to the job. You secure the information by asking open-ended questions and steering the interview through the topics that are relative to the job under consideration. Keep in mind as you ask your questions that the person doing the most talking is the one being interviewed ... the interviewee can be sitting on either side of the desk. The interview is a hunting process for sure. You are hunting for the best employment match, and to do it right you need to hunt for positive traits or skills as well as negative ones. It is easy to discover the good side of a job candidate as it is handed to you in the form of a resume or an application. A skilled interviewer needs to find out the negative side of the candidate as well. To interview well you must be a good hunter.

Here too beware of what I will call "The First Five." By that I mean to beware of making your decision based primarily on the first five steps the candidate takes, the first five minutes of the interview, the first five things the candidate says, or the first five questions you ask. As an example of the first five influence, think about a job candidate that you have interviewed where the candidate was not skilled in interviewing and was very anxious or nervous throughout the interview. The nervousness may have caused the candidate to verbally stumble when answering questions, causing you to dismiss him or her from consideration. This person may still have been an excellent match for the job at hand. Conversely, if you interview a person skilled in interviewing (maybe me), the responses to your questions would not carry the same delays or nervousness but the candidate could be a poor job match. Do not be unduly influenced (plus or minus) by the first five, and do a good job of interviewing. I believe most employment decisions are made based almost entirely on some component of the first five; consequently the balance of the interview time is taken only to secure support for the decision made at the very beginning. The first five seconds of a meeting may work out well in a romance novel but serves very little purpose in a job interview. Interviewing is not easy and few people do it well.

After a job candidate is identified, the most important step in the employment selection process is to do good reference checks. Reference checks take time but are easy to do, and you will discover more about a job candidate doing reference checks than you will ever discover in a job interview. The goal with reference checks is no different than the interview itself and that is three-fold:

1. Can the candidate do the job?
2. Will the candidate do the job if they have it?
3. Will this candidate fit into the character, chemistry, and culture of your organization?

I know that many or possibly most employment decisions are made without reference checking and some HR folks even claim they do not need to do reference checks as they possess such great interview skills... maybe yes and maybe no. I have interviewed tens of thousands of job candidates, and consider myself very good at it however I always complete reference checks. Let me also submit that on occasion reference checking did not support my interview decision. Remember most interview decisions are based on the first five which is not a reliable basis for decisions regarding your organizations human asset requirements… ultimately your companies future.

By policy your organization should require a minimum of two reference checks, a school check (high schools are great sources of information), and a work reference check. It is easy to do this and can be partially automated with a computer. You need to require that all applicants complete and sign an employment application. Above the applicant's signature, place a paragraph or two that clearly states that the information on the application is true and that the applicant's signature (or photo copy of) provides a full release to verify any information contained in the application.

As a side note, I have noticed, over the years, there are two things job applicants are most inclined to be dishonest about, and those two things are earnings and education. A little fudge job on earnings is no big deal, however I cannot tell you how often I have uncovered significant dishonesty regarding educational achievements. The applicants may state that they have a college degree, and they do not. They may claim to have graduated from high school, and they did not. Or they may claim to have an advanced university degree and yet may never have attended a university. I think this academic dishonesty, in part, goes back to the normal/average and IQ thing.

Get to know high school counselors in your recruiting area as well as records office personnel from the various colleges and universities that provide you with employment candidates. Have their FAX numbers and e-mails handy, then get a copy of the applicant's release sent to the school immediately after the interview. College and high school transcripts contain an immense amount of relevant job performance information - information that you can never get out of an interview no matter how skilled you are.

High school attendance records are an important component of a grade transcript, and I have found it generally true that the attendance patterns developed by a person in high school generally follow him or her through life. Some high school counselors have even advised me that they do not get concerned (from a truancy standpoint) about missed school days until the student misses twenty or more days.

Now think about this for a moment: Can your organization operate effectively if everyone misses an extra twenty days? Also, the school year is based on 180 days or forty percent less than your business year. Consequently using an apples-to-apples comparison a twenty-day high school absentee would really be missing an additional thirty days a year at work. Turnover and problems related to unexcused absenteeism are primarily caused by a poor employee selection process (the basics of HR). Those problems can be very expensive for business and impossible to correct in a work setting. Watch those expenses, and keep operating costs down to help attract customer dollars - it's the customer, the customer, the customer.

College transcripts can provide a wealth of job related information on the candidate's drive, direction, and motivation as well as academic strengths. How long did it take the candidate to complete a four-year degree? How disciplined was he or she in addressing the school's curriculum? A treasure trove of information is contained in a college transcript and the cost to secure it is little or nothing. This information can also assist in structuring follow-up candidate interviews.

With reference checks keep in mind that even if the person failed in a past occupational assignment that failure does not necessarily mean that they will fail in every future assignment. Some work relationships simply do not unfold favorably for reasons beyond the control of the job candidate (hey, I had one, maybe you too). A past unsuccessful endeavor does not automatically imply that the candidate's work performance will fail in your organization. A reference check is simply a selection tool that validates, and provides information. It is your obligation to use that information wisely and legally.

I mention legally because there are organizations harboring fears of post-employment litigation if they give out job/work information (certainly negative information). These organizations have consequently written policies stating employment reference checks will not be provided even if the request is accompanied by a signed release from the individual. It is my belief that the reference check litigation fear is not well-founded. In fact the opposite can be true if you withhold information about illegal and/or deviant behavior that you are aware of that may have resulted in disciplinary measures or a forced termination. If given a signed release and you provide honest information (even limited information) and document what transpired, you should have no problem. Also, if your organization has a restrictive reference check policy in place, keep this in mind: I have never been unable to secure the reference checks I needed on any job candidate no matter what the candidate's past company policy was – never. While aggravating, it only took me a little more time. Your organizations future is best served by securing reference checks before an employment offer is made and by providing (with documentation) reference checks on past employees.

A sound employment program with good selection tools will help curb the costs associated with turnover, and those costs can be real business killers. I once met a manager of a large discount department store and (as is my practice) asked questions about his HR issues. On turnover, he said that annual turnover at his store exceeded 300 percent. Turnover was so bad that it created problems with the work-skill trainers who became so overburdened with work that they quit in droves. He had to establish a program to train the trainers so as to train the unending revolving door of new workers. Man, this guy had problems. Turnover, voluntary and involuntary, can be a killer, driving up your costs and lowering productivity.

Let me also add that with new hires don't miss the opportunity on the first day of employment to get things started right. Good new-hire orientation programs are, sadly, rare. Set up a comprehensive "beginning employment" package and follow through with each new employee. Organizations will never have a better chance to influence a worker more than on the first day of employment. Let new employees know what your organization is, how it operates and where it's going. Capture this time to assure a positive start. The most common gripe I've heard from workers at all levels centers on the "baptismal-fire" scenario. "They (management) just put me on the job and didn't tell me much of anything." Generally in manufacturing situations a union steward will step forward and do the job that should have been done by management. You see, the union steward serves as a guide when management fails.

If your company is non-union and you want to stay that way, say so right up front. I worked with a labor lawyer once who had been engaged in a number of union organizing drives. He told me that surprisingly he often heard from workers being organized that they were not aware the company did not want a union. Crazy, management goes to great lengths to challenge a union drive, spending large sums of money on litigation yet failed to tell employees how they wanted to operate. If your organization does not want third party intervention, say so right up front. On the first day of employment try saying something like this: "We at Company M are not unionized. We deal with our workforce honestly and fairly and do not think a third party (union) is needed.

We will do everything legally possible to avoid unionization." Just a straight forward message delivered at a time when management has influential leverage (communicate – be a guide).

Starting off on the right foot is important and employment continuity can be improved by interviewing departing workers. Exit interviews are important. When exiting an organization, for any reason, an employee will talk more candidly about change recommendations. These departing recommendations (beyond: *take this job and shove it*) often prove beneficial for both organizational development and individual manager development programs.

Key points and final comments on this subject:

- Recognize that recruiting is HR's most important endeavor and give that responsibility the most attention.
- Utilize all selection tools available to you including outside support services and measure the results (SPC) of tools and services employed.
- This is the greatest area where HR serves as both hunter and guide building a future for the business enterprise.

On the subject of involuntary turnover, let me now say a few words about synergy.

SYNERGY

Historically, career employment with an established organization was almost a given, and the job match discipline was aimed toward long term employee/employer relationships. Recruiters looked for people who had a stable employment record, indicating that this prospective employee might join and then stay with the organization for a career, not for short time employment. Much of that has changed, and today

HR professionals are called on to recruit employees, knowing that a long term employment scenario will not unfold. In many cases it is almost like a day work scenario for professionals.

Going forward individuals will need to change jobs more often to keep their careers on track and preserve employment continuity. Current estimates conclude that workers will be changing jobs every three to five years throughout their career. Historically multiple job changes were viewed negatively by interviewers as it reflected some potential work instability that would compound turnover and increase costs. Today the story is different as job changes are expected. Within this recruiting chaos, HR departments must also be prepared to handle what I call constructive synergy or the need to plan, communicate, and implement ever-changing staffing requirements.

These synergy changes are not all bad as some organizations truly need to address over staffing issues (hopefully the Federal Government). I attended a staffing/HR seminar once lead by Dr. Lawrence L. Steinmetz, PhD and at this seminar Dr. Steinmetz shared a true story about overstaffing and business performance. In the case he sited, an acquaintance of his purchased a small manufacturing business that employed around two-hundred people. Upon acquisition the buyer hoped to improve on the businesses performance, as it had been operating in the red. After considerable management effort on his part, he was wholly unsuccessful and the business continued to operate in the red. The business buyer got so frustrated that he initiated what was called "The Parking Lot Philosophy." One morning he ordered all two-hundred employees into the parking lot and told them they were all fired. He also told them that he would call them back to work as their skills were needed. Initially the business buyer did recall a dozen or so workers needed immediately as orders had to be shipped, telephones answered etc. He continued to recall workers as needed and soon the business was out of the red and running very smoothly. The significance of this story is that, in this particular situation, the owner called back fewer than one-hundred of the two-hundred workers ordered into the parking lot. His parking lot philosophy may have created a mass of unhappy people but, in this situation, the company survived a pending doom. Business failure would have resulted in even more unhappy people. Synergy change still carries a heavy human price tag.

Abraham Maslow was a behavioral scientist who developed a hierarchy-of-needs philosophy, appropriately called: "Maslow's needs hierarchy." This hierarchical philosophy was cleverly represented using a triangular graph. This graph delineated changing needs with basic survival needs at the base of the triangle, increasing to safety needs, then social needs, on to Ego needs and finally the need for self-actualization --- the peak of the triangle. Maslow's theory of needs hierarchy gained world-wide recognition and acceptance (including mine) even though I cannot say that it was ever scientifically tested. Today, with the great number of synergy plans unfolding, a scientific test would require a measure of accountability factoring in legions of managers who were operating at Maslow's peak, self-actualizing to beat the band, who suddenly (as in the parking lot philosophy) got shoved back to the bottom of the hierarchy searching for basic or safety needs. Times are changing and it is not all fun.

At the beginning of this book I mentioned the news release regarding a major pharmaceutical corporation buying a prescription drug company where the two organizations claimed that they will gain four-hundred million in "operating synergies." Included in that four-hundred million would be many job eliminations, and everyone working in both organizations knows this will happen. Some of those individuals will stay, and some will not. Some corporate departments will stay and some will not. Some physical locations will close, and some will not as the synergy process unfolds. One true certainty is that productivity in both organizations has now taken a back seat and will stay there until the synergy dust settles. The second true certainty is that individual productivity will never fully recover. The newly synergized organization will have fewer people and fewer payroll dollars, but it will never be the same. Employees (staying and leaving) subjected to the synergy process feel betrayed and never forget. Let me say that a second time . . . they never forget!

Synergizing will always leave you with turnover expenses that can be killers. It comes in basically two forms. First are the expenses associated with those who quit or terminate and leave (replacement, job coverage, training, etc.). Second is the more insidious form of turnover expense which is incurred by those who quit and stay. I will submit that the second form of turnover is much more expensive.

I have taken part in synergizing a few organizations in my career, and one thing that always amazed me was how often key executives would later complain to me about lack of worker loyalty. Loyalty you see, is a two-way street.

The ongoing change process HR professionals face today is not easy. You might ask: "Hey, Bill, you've done many, so what is the best way to prepare and process a personnel synergy plan?"

"I don't know the best."

I personally believe that while loyalty and job security may have been relegated to the history books of management, a productive employee relationship can still be established. To do this management must be honest with their employees regarding business circumstances (good and bad), and management must endeavor to deliver satisfying work. My late father told me that if you were honest about what you were doing, and always did your level best that you would never need to look back with regret. That philosophy certainly holds true in this new synergized employment relationship.

Key points and final comments on this subject:
- Recognize that we live in a world economy and respond to those changes (be a hunter).
- Communicate to your workers directly and honestly (be a guide).
- Do your level best to deliver satisfying work (be a guide).

TESTING

For selection assistance, I recommend both functional and psychological testing. Testing not only serves as a selection tool (remember it is only a tool), it sends a message throughout your organization that you have high work standards and want the best candidates to join the best team.

What initiated my interest in functional testing happened years ago when I was recruiting production workers and sadly discovered that many students graduating from high school were not able to read a simple ruler or do basic math. On my first (self-developed) math test, the most difficult question, certainly the one missed most often, was a simple ruler question. On the test form, I copied a six-inch ruler, and the question asked was a two part question: Part A. Find and mark with an "X" 1 3/8 inches. Part B. Find and mark with an "X" 2 5/8 inches. Applicants' inability to answer this question or perform simple math was appalling and compelled me to start a basic math class for employees at work. I hired a math teacher who, during his summer vacation, taught basic math to our employees. This program was incorporated into a Statistical Process Control (SPC) format, in part as a shield for any embarrassment a worker might have regarding his/her limited math skill and more importantly to promote the concepts embraced in SPC. The training results from this basic skill training program were all very positive for both the employees in the program and the company.

Private companies may consider it a waste of time providing education in basic learning areas missed by public schools, nevertheless these skills may be lacking in the organization. Those missing skills consistently drag down work performance - simple as that. Noted football coach Vince Lombardi once said, "It all starts with knowing the basics." Football basics are blocking and tackling. Business basics are reading, writing and arithmetic. If basic job skills aren't present, they need to be developed.

STRENGHT TESTS

Some time back I worked for two years as the employment manager at a steel mill in Ohio, and I found that the steel mill culture was pretty well set in its reactionary way when it came to hiring female workers (and other matters). Trying to get female employment candidates a fair shot at the factory jobs was a daunting task. The irony here was that this plant had been built at the start of World War II and due to wartime labor shortages, most of the jobs in this steel mill were held by female workers. The steel production requirements during the war were demanding, and the female workforce did a fine job making and delivering products in all areas of the steel mill. After the war these women surrendered their jobs to the men returning home as it was socially accepted in 1945 that these were "men-only" jobs. Forty years later, not much had changed at this steel company, and female workers were profoundly underutilized throughout the mill.

My supervisor at the time was a guy named Jim Rimmel. Jim was VPHR and a very bright guy, fully supportive of equal opportunity in all areas of employment, including being very sensitive to the underutilization of females. The old-guard of the mill (superintendents, general foreman, supervisors) were reluctant to add female workers. The standard gripe from them was that women couldn't do steel mill work because the work was too physically demanding (Remember Hilda?). It was a ridiculous complaint, but to counter that bias, Jim worked with an outside agency to set up strength testing and requisite standards for our mill. At first I was opposed to these strength tests as I doubted that they could be made valid, reliable, or job related in the eyes of governmental regulating agencies (not to mention these tests would take a ton of my time and require a lot of extra work). I envisioned myself spending endless hours before various civil rights groups defending the company right to employ these tests.

As it turned out, my doubts proved to be unfounded. The strength tests did not disproportionately screen out female workers and proved to be a very valid and reliable selection tool. In fact, one of the most outspoken critics of hiring females was a shop superintendent, a person of significant influence in the organization, who had been trying to get me to hire one of his relatives, a brother-in-law as I remember. I interviewed the brother-in-law and found him to be a horrible job candidate in every way, and yet the superintendent was unrelenting in his insistence that this male relative be hired (also that HR stop trying to force him to hire physically weak and unqualified female workers).

Jim's strength testing came along and guess what? The female candidates applying for mill work had no problem passing the strength tests, but the superintendent's brother-in-law failed all four parts of the test! I just loved the results!

Jim Rimmel recognized that sometimes you have to go that extra mile to get the job done right.

Here is my point; Strength testing, if needed, can be set-up in a way that is job related, valid and reliable. In addition, candidates applying for those positions (male and female) will generally bring with them the adequate physical skills to perform the job.

TEAM TESTING

Team-testing is also important in most job settings, as you need to bring working talent into the organization, and those workers must be willing to work as a team. Here I have to say that the Toyota Manufacturing plant in Kentucky does a remarkable job. The Toyota selection process is very well designed and aimed at getting the right match between worker interests, ability, and the job requirements. The Toyota program includes work skill evaluations in an on-the-job setting before a candidate is even considered for employment. Only approximately nine percent of the job applicants make it through the sophisticated selection process at Toyota. It is not that the rejected ninety-one percent represents a collection of bad people, only that they are not believed to be a match for the work design of an automobile assembly line.

Now, compare this selection process to the process employed by manufacturing plant of another car maker I am personally familiar with and will call Company Z. The Company Z plant employs thousands of workers, has union representation and a deplorable counter productive labor relations history from its beginning. Most of us in HR would describe labor relations at this plant to be a total nightmare that includes many cases of product sabotage on the assembly line by represented hourly employees. The car they were assembling was a bad enough car on its own and didn't need destructive assistance from disgruntled employees. It is unconscionable to me to know that employees would deliberately destroy the products coming down the assembly line, but they did at Company Z. These workers were obviously ones who represented a poor job match (at best). I remember when Company Z's management added an entire third shift, several hundred workers, to the workforce, and they completed the entire employment project over a weekend! Getting hired at Toyota might take ten to twelve months, but getting hired at Company Z was a two-day selection process. As managers, we often create our own people problems, and Company Z turned that problem creation process into an art form. Hiring hundreds of workers over a two-day time frame is a little too near-sighted for me, and, I believe, Company Z's management was, no doubt, responsible for selecting a few saboteurs. My bet is that Company Z's management would have probably examined a physical asset purchase (like a $10,000 cut-off saw) in great detail but were happy to direct instant results when they added an entire new shift to the workforce. You financial folks keep in mind that this happened back at the same time that I added twenty-five hourly workers (at a lower wage & benefit rate), and those twenty-five represented a cost of nearly a million dollars. In this example, Company Z may have literally thrown away close to $100 million, and remember, all dollars are customer dollars.

One other interesting component of the employment relationship at Toyota in Kentucky was the termination/separation arrangement that was described to me. All steps of the disciplinary process at Toyota were focused on correction. This focus was influenced in part by the time and money tied up in securing a fully trained worker. It was too expensive to be casual regarding discharge. The final step in the process included a peer review or appeal prior to implementing discharge. The Toyota management representative I was with advised that thirty percent of the termination decisions implemented by management were reversed by this peer review committee, and while management could override these peer review reversal decisions, they had never overridden a single one. You see, the system had integrity. The Toyota management representative also advised me that all of the reinstatements made by peer review committees were accompanied by a qualifier. As example, with a poor attendance situation the peer review reinstatement might carry a mandatory discharge without appeal if the worker missed another day. Interesting, because it is clear that other team members at Toyota recognized that they were all on the same team and everyone needed to play by the same rules.

I have to wonder what a peer committee would have done with my rat shooting discharge.

I take my hat off to the management folks at Toyota in Kentucky.

Key points and final comments on this subject:
- Recognize that testing can be an effective support tool, but only a tool.
- Employ tests that have job relevance and do so judiciously (be the hunter, be the guide).
- Measure results of testing (SPC) – test the tests.

PHYSICALLY DISABLED WORKERS

Hiring physically disabled workers is more than just a good idea. Give a high priority to hiring the physically disabled but avoid hiring the unhealthy (there is a difference). Remember my Ercoupe pilot example? That was just one example, from millions, that manifests how physically disabled workers can bring a determination to succeed with them to the job coupled with a lasting appreciation for the opportunity to work that you cannot find elsewhere. Conversely, unhealthy people, those who do not take care of their physical well being (e.g. chain cigarette smokers) will only drive up your business costs and lower your productivity. Do not misunderstand me here regarding physically disabled/handicapped employment but do keep in mind your cost of doing business. At my last employer, our group health cost rose to over $12,000 per year per employee which, by the way, converts to $6.00 per hour for all hours paid. HR managers need to keep a focus on wages paid for time worked and not worked, and must always keep the competition in mind. If your competition is coming from China the total benefit cost there averages only twenty-eight cents per hour, and that is one big cost delta.

Key points and final comments on this subject:
- Recognize that physically handicapped workers can represent a positive and productive talent when recruiting (hunting & guiding).
- Keep health care costs down by avoiding cigarette smokers when recruiting.

DIVERSITY

"I am free of all prejudices.
I hate everyone equally."

W.C. Fields

It is critical for the success of your business to hire and maintain a diverse workforce. Forget fair employment laws, the litigation mania, and governmental punishment scenarios for a moment, and think about your business and its future. Diversity in employment brings with it new ideas, new insight, and the power of vast experience to the work place that will benefit your operation and the bottom line. Diversity can be a true blessing to your company. You will fail if you overlook the richness of this human resource. Also, it is important to recognize that your customers both here and overseas are a very diverse collection of people. Remember it is the customers: customers, customers, customers!

Please make yourself aware that steep legal penalties are in place and waiting for you if your company violates protected employment rights. I will reserve that litigation topic for another book.

Key points and final comments on this subject:

- Recognize that diversity brings unimaginable talent to the work force.
- Know that this may be the most demanding area for hunting and guiding.
- Measure your recruiting results (SPC) to assure compliance to law and business ethics.
- Remember that your customers are very diversified

PERFORMANCE APPRAISALS

Earlier I mentioned how difficult it is to give honest feedback to workers in a formal evaluation setting and the "drift", if you will, of evaluations toward the high side of the scale (nobody wants to be called average). I also mentioned a legal case that was lost where the company performance appraisal documents actually hurt their case. That particular legal case was filed as a charge of age discrimination. Now, this company had historically, and unknowingly, allowed supervisors and managers to place statements in performance appraisal documents that were not job relevant and reflected an age bias. Statements such as: "Bob is well suited on this job for his age" and "Sam will probably stay on this job until retirement" were found throughout the performance appraisal documents. While I am confident that those comments were not intended as age bias, the court's interpretation was, and those comments proved to be the loaded gun that cost this company over twelve million dollars.

To help avoid drift bias and legal problems with performance appraisals I can only recommend that HR departments advise and train managers to adhere to the four important points listed below

Performance Appraisal Guide

1. Be Objective and Timely.
2. Set Goals and Standards.
3. Be Honest and Consistent.
4. Use Accurate and Job-Relevant Documentation.

Key points and final comments on this subject:
*   Measure key managers and supervisors on how well they conduct performance appraisals.
*   Give serious thought to ranking (top to bottom) all workers and include some form of peer evaluation.
*   Guiding skills here are critical.

Union/labor Relations

This is an ingredient of HR that has seen monumental change over the last two decades. Early in my career, labor relations skills were a critical component of the HR discipline. Labor relations and union negotiations were areas of HR that commanded most of your attention if you worked in a third party represented organization (unionized shop). To be successful you had to be able to understand and work within the structure of a unionized work setting. Today, it is much less so as third party (union) membership continues to decline, and represented workers are fewer each year as a percentage of the total workforce. New union organizing drives fail with regularity, and sadly, many represented businesses have disappeared never to return. Unions continue to play an important role in the way businesses manage (or mismanage) their human assets. With your workforce, be aware that unions are ever-present, standing at the ready, to counter management incompetence or dishonesty.

It is my opinion that the primary reason we have unions and those onerous federal and state labor laws has been and continues to be bad management and/or corporate abuse. A need for unions came about to balance the scale with management and bring reason to the employer/employee relationship. Some might argue that the scale has tipped decidedly in favor of unions, and in some major industries, union power, arrogance and near sightedness has been able to match that of uncontrolled corporate America. True or not, no reasonable person can argue that labor unions did not step forward to fill a critical need.

My grandfather was killed at work when the construction scaffolding he was working from collapsed at his job site. His death happened before the National Labor Relations Act was passed or Social Security implemented. In those days, when a worker was killed on the job, he was quickly replaced and the family of the worker only notified that they needed to make arrangements to take care of their loved one. The loss of the primary bread winner in any family then and now is catastrophic, and for my father's family this was certainly true. Dad was very young when his father was killed, and later, when he was able, Dad took a job delivering telegrams on his bicycle for seventeen cents an hour to help support his mother and sisters. Then at age fifteen, he quit school and took a full-time job driving a coal truck for a few more cents an hour.

Unions helped fill a need, and they did so very well.

For an overall philosophy on union relations I have to think back to a meeting with a man named Russ Mavis in the early 1970s. Russ was a bright guy, very experienced in labor relations, and a real dynamo at work. His job at the time was corporate labor relations manager (or something like that), and we were working together preparing our company case for a number of grievances that a local union of the United Steel Workers of America (USWA) had referred to the arbitration step of the grievance procedure. The local union representatives at this manufacturing site were a misguided collection of misfits who dominated the local union political scene, and would send grievances to arbitration by the dozen, regardless of merit and void of reason.

When I asked Russ what his philosophy was on union relations he responded that I should look at it in very basic terms: "You have the givers and the takers." Then he added, "If the givers give too much then both sides lose."

You may or may not like Russ's philosophy, but he made a very good point. Reflect on it for a moment because maybe, just maybe, some U.S. businesses (major U.S. corporations) are in deep trouble today because historically management was willing to give away too much as a way to appease their labor unions, settle a strike, or attempt to secure third party cooperation. You see a capitulation mentality on the part of management can carry with it a very steep price. Short term thinking always generates long term grief and those higher labor costs, increased manning requirements, and restrictive work rules place a company in a position where it simply cannot compete. Capitulation can provide short-term relief that builds into a long-term disaster.

Management and union leaders in represented organizations (private and public) need to be much more realistic and responsible in their dealings with one another to survive. Both sides must remember that they have customers who pay all the bills, and there are customers in the public sector as well. For government workers, your customers are called taxpayers. In any of your represented organizations it might be advantageous to give thought to what Russ Mavis said to me so many years ago. "If you give too much, both sides lose."

At the beginning of this book I said that I would speak with truth and, in truth, third party representation consistently steers a fixed course toward higher costs and work performance mediocrity - period.

Business leaders as well as their HR managers need to keep in mind that third party representation can be avoided but only through responsible people management practices, simple as that.

Before I leave the topic of labor unions, let me give any management readers something additional to think about. There were times in manufacturing when I had to meet with supervisors or managers who were having colossal difficulty grasping even the basics of good human relations. Remember, management too often can be its own worst enemy. To help out these recalcitrant managers/supervisors, I would give them, now get this as it is true, a copy of the <u>American Federation of Labor and Congress of Industrial Organizations (AFL-CIO) Manual for Shop Stewards</u> and make them read it. If managers cannot responsibly manage their human assets, there are people out there who can "help." The AFL-CIO is one of those organizations. Let me add this AFL-CIO booklet contains some great people management ideas. It serves as a good guide, you see.

Key points and final comments on this subject:

- Recognize (admit) that unions are here because bad management was/is present and remove those bad management practices.
- Keep in mind (like it or not) that in the labor relations world you have the givers and the takers.
- Hunting skills in labor relations can be demanding and guiding through this litigation maze is tough to master.

BENEFITS AND COMPENSATION

This is a critical HR area, and it is a very high cost area. The HR department has a responsibility to design benefit and compensation programs needed to attract and retain talent and be able to control the ever escalating benefit expenses. You might say they are mutually exclusive activities because attracting talent with a good benefits and compensation package may generate higher costs, which then requires new cost control measures. Implementing cost control measures often results in the reduction or elimination of components of that benefit package -- something of a vicious circle. I didn't say that good work performance in HR was easy.

GROUP HEALTH INSURANCE

Benefits management is clearly an area of big bucks and potentially big grief. In the insurance arena I referred to most group health products as "Big Losers". All the other insurance products were relatively easy to manage but not group health. My company had evolved into a more senior organization (average age in our industry was around thirty-two, and ours hovered near the mid forties). Older workers generate higher health costs. Saying that is not age discrimination . . . it's a truth, a fact. Our group insurance product costs were increasing each year by percentages well into the double digits, with our retirement plans leading the way delivering astounding increases (increases that might send your CFO to an early grave). Keep in mind that health insurance cost increases are caused by more than just inflation. Health costs have risen due to what is referred to as "trend" which includes: inflation, new technology applications, increased service utilization, cost shifting to private plans, and, of course, legal. Too often it is the litigation engine that drives the entire package up.

One example of cost shifting that amazed me happened several years ago when I was working to set up a preferred provider contract at a hospital, in a small midwest city. This hospital was operating at a steep loss and very reluctant to enter into any managed care discounting contract. Part of the financial loss they suffered was due to cost-shifting from non-paying customers (uninsured and unable to pay) to paying customers (me and my company). This hospital told me that their uncollectible invoices ran at well over twent-six percent of total billing. Wow! Try to put that cost into your business, and then shift it onto other customers – a nightmare at best.

Retired numbers at my last company were at the four-to-one level (four retired individuals for every active), far worse than social security statistics. Let me add that costs for company health insurance plans covering our Canadian personnel were increasing by 200 to 300 percent a year (this, at a time when many US politicians were touting the benefits of Canadian health insurance). No one was ever happy with the coverage or the costs involved when I managed this complex and expensive monster. The hospitals didn't like what I was doing, employees didn't like what I was doing, the doctors didn't like what I was doing, the insurance providers didn't like what I was doing, the retirees didn't like what I was doing, my company didn't like what I was doing (health care expenditures continued to accelerate), and when I came home at night, my wife let me know that she didn't like what I was doing! For me it was the big loser, and no matter what I did to structure a competitive health care plan, my actions were never viewed with favor. Health insurance plan management was always a thankless endeavor in my HR days.

Once, a retired company HR director invited my boss and I to a lunch meeting with a group of retirees (I was director of benefits at the time). This HR director had retired from one of the company divisions that happened to represent a very senior group of people (even measured by our standards) and, consequently, had a very large retiree population. The lunch was a regular Tuesday affair and held in an informal setting at a restaurant convenient to most of the retired workers. I was working on a number of possible retiree health plan changes at the time and sending out the initial notification correspondence to the covered groups of retirees. This retired HR director was fully aware of the need to make health care changes and even thought the changes that I had under consideration were a little on the light side. He said it might be good for us to meet with this group, first hand, to explain the "why" behind the contemplated health coverage changes. Great idea! My boss and I jumped at the opportunity. Now, this retiree lunch meeting was a casual, loosely structured, affair that generally attracted around twenty to thirty people (a BYO type of arrangement), but there were more than one hundred retirees present at this one because word spread fast that we would be there to talk about health insurance (touchy issue for retired folks). The restaurant was jam packed.

My boss, Joe Huss, took the lead in this meeting and he did an excellent job of describing the retiree health insurance situation, doing so in a way that nearly everyone present appreciated and acknowledged that changes were needed and that the measures we proposed were not really that dramatic. They didn't like it, but they understood things much better knowing the "why" behind the changes. Nevertheless, there were still some meeting participants who remained very bitter about the changes, believing they were entitled to lifetime health care benefits once they retired.

One of those disgruntled retirees was sitting directly across the table from me. She was a senior retired person and, while of small stature, had a very loud voice, and I suspect poor hearing. After Joe finished his presentation, he opened the meeting to questions, and the first question came from this woman, who obviously had not heard our introductions. She asked Joe, in her very loud voice, "Mister, I understand what you are saying, but what I want to know is just who the hell is this damned guy named Bill Wonders!" Cripe, it turned out I was sitting smack in the middle of a lion's den. When it finally ended, I felt like the coyote at the conclusion of a Road Runner Cartoon. There were days in my career when I can truly say that I more than earned my pay, and this was one of those days.

"The secret of managing
is to keep the guys who hate you
away from the guys who are undecided."

Casey Stengel

Whatever you HR/Benefit folks are doing today regarding future health care cost control and/or plan design change for group health insurance plans, I can only say, "Good luck."

The big plus for me when I was working with group health plans, possibly the single bright light, was having an opportunity, starting in the early part of my benefits work, to align myself with two truly outstanding people: John Cree and Terry McManamon. John and Terry were professional consultants I contracted with who can only be described as excellent advisors (great hunters and great guides) who went above and beyond the call of duty to get things done. They were incredibly bright and just fun people to work with. Together we were, without question, the avant-garde of managed care programs and experimental leaders in new plan design. John, Terry, and later, Megan Kelly (a new consultant working for them) were individuals who consistently accomplished the impossible regarding administration of group health insurance plans. We negotiated and set up preferred provider networks in areas of the country that had never even heard that terminology employed. We were at the front of the line when it came to implementing managed care plans and new, cost control, plan design measures. In Canada we were even able to bring some semblance of control over the quantum increases thrown at us by the Canadian

Government's health plan cost-shifting onto the private sector. No, for me, work in group health was not fun; it was hard, demanding, unappreciated work, yet working with these great folks made things so much better. They were three special people who had a knack for making difficult work fun, and I will be forever in their debt.

I never fully realized how much was accomplished, with their help, until much later, at a meeting of top HRVP's and HR Directors in Cleveland, Ohio. The agenda for this meeting was focused on what could be done to control increasing health insurance costs (certainly a subject of interest to me). I realized, in that meeting, all the cost control ideas that this group had under consideration (new to them), were programs and plan design projects that we had already tried and/or implemented throughout North America. John, Terry and Megan were three positive people, and together we positively got things done.

Now, you might ask, "Hey Bill, you have done all these health insurance control things, how about taking a job at my company to help us control our future health insurance cost(s)?"

My answer is an unqualified NO! You see, Bill's done getting beat up by old ladies.

"The future ain't what it used to be."

Yogi Berra

Key points and final comments on this subject:
- Remember that customer dollars pay all the business costs and group insurance is a very large cost.
- Do not hesitate to test new plan designs for cost control and health care service delivery (hunt).
- Aggressively employ professional outside services and measure the service performance (SPC) [guide].

WORKERS COMPENSATION

Before leaving the domain of big losers let me take a moment to comment on workers compensation. Yes, when it comes to health insurance, the king of big losers has to be workers compensation no matter where you do your business. Some states manage workers compensation better than others, but in the aggregate it is a program in desperate need of repair or replacement (my vote is for replacement). The regulation was initially designed to curb company abuses of work-injured employees, and employers accepted it because, in the beginning, it was the sole remedy for work related injuries (that protection has changed). Over time the sole remedy protection has eroded away in the courts and gradually the workers compensation program became an administrative nightmare as well as a legal and costly behemoth. The added costs to business from the workers compensation system have single handedly sent companies on the run from state to state and overseas. I know of a company in Ohio that closed three work sites and moved to Kentucky where workers compensation costs were more reasonable, and the workers compensation cost savings alone justified this major business relocation. Intel Corporation has been open about their interest in placing new plants outside of California because the California workers compensation system (arguably the worst out of all fifty states) is so expensive and an onerous burden for business. I worked for a company president once who had a site location philosophy he called "ABC" --- an acronym for Anyplace But California.

I shut down a company in California years ago that had as part of its business a manufacturing location that had been closed many years earlier. This location had no active workers and no active compensation claims or any claims eligible for reactivation (deadlines to reopen old claims had expired) yet the state of California required my company to place nearly 250,000 dollars in a restricted savings account to pay "potential" future claims. My company was given no access to those assets and the money had to stay in this do-nothing account for seventy-five years before it would be returned – an absolutely ludicrous requirement. Hey, that's California.

Left unchecked and unchallenged, the workers compensation program can become an expensive problem, a cancer that simply feeds on itself. HR must stay on top of all costs associated with workers compensation. HR representatives must thoroughly investigate every claim filed, challenge fraudulent claims, and attend every scheduled hearing on those claims. Most important the HR department must work directly with general management to help create a work site free of injuries. No one wins when a worker gets injured.

As I now reflect back on the enormous cost of workers compensation I think a separate book is needed. I will need to think real hard about tackling that one. Maybe I'll write a book on the subject and place a photograph of the HMS Titanic on its cover.

Key points and final comments on this subject:
- Stay on top of worker's compensation costs, attend all hearings, challenge questionable claims. Be aggressive in your administration of this business obligation (hunt).
- Employ outside professional support services and measure their performance (SPC) [guide].

PENSIONS

Competent pension management demands that the practitioner understand the legal and philosophical history of pension evolution. Recognize too that a heightened level of program interest exists because no person on earth can be indifferent when it comes to post-work income. Recognize that the need for retirement protection is simply universal.

In the U.S., individual thrift and savings have been preached to us from the start by notables such as Statesman Benjamin Franklin with his oft quoted: "A penny saved is a penny earned" message. Individuals living through the Great Depression have been more influenced to save than others since that time, but as a nation, we do recognize the need to save for retirement. Now if you compare U.S. savings rates with Japan or Western Europe, the U.S. savings rate is very low. Individual savings, as a percent of income, in those countries resides in the double digits while U.S. individual saving, as a percent of income, rests in the low to mid single digits. The U.S. has historically been a spending culture versus savings culture, but today and moving forward that will change.

In Attachment I, I have briefly summarized key U.S. pension changes dating back to our nation's beginning. This overall summary is interesting because viewing this chronological bar graph, there appear to be two key historical periods of change regarding U.S. pension evolution and development. The first significant period took place in the pre World War II and post World War II time frame (This had to have been, in part, influenced by the many sacrifices made by people during the long period of economic depression). At this time private pensions received a big boost with the passing of the National Labor Relations Act (1935) and then a requirement for national pensions was addressed with the subsequent passing of the Social Security Act that same year. These two laws certainly set the wheels in motion for U.S. pension evolution. The second period, in my opinion, was the time frame when "baby boomers" started to think about retirement. Ideas came to the fore during this second period that established tax-deferred pension plans, and a national conscience unfolded that added legal protection for private pension plans.

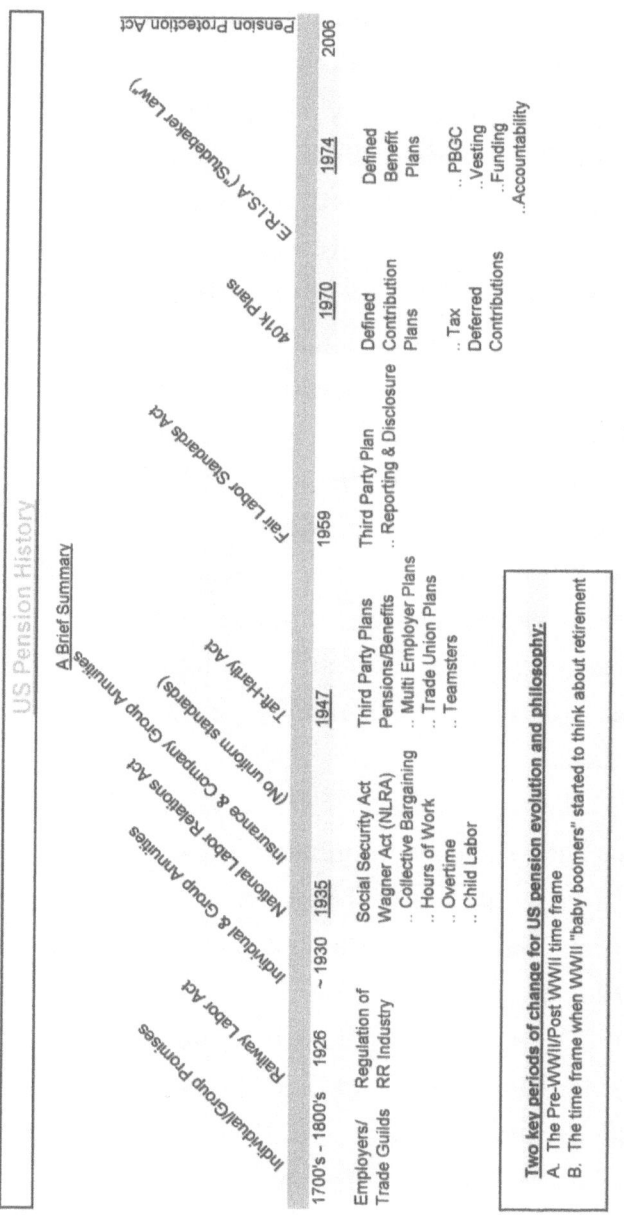

The following content appears within the timeline figure:

US Pension History

A Brief Summary

1700's - 1800's	1926	~ 1930	1935	1947	1959	1970	1974	2006

Individual/Group Promises — Railway Labor Act — Individual & Group Annuities — National Labor Relations Act — Insurance & Company/Group Annuities (No uniform standards) — Taft-Hardy Act — Fair Labor Standards Act — 401k Plans — E.R.I.S.A ("Studebaker Law") — Pension Protection Act

| Employers/ Trade Guilds | Regulation of RR Industry | | Social Security Act Wagner Act (NLRA) .. Collective Bargaining .. Hours of Work .. Overtime .. Child Labor | Third Party Plans Pensions/Benefits .. Multi Employer Plans .. Trade Union Plans .. Teamsters | Third Party Plan .. Reporting & Disclosure | Defined Contribution Plans ..Tax Deferred Contributions | Defined Benefit Plans ..PBGC ..Vesting ..Funding ..Accountability | |

Two key periods of change for US pension evolution and philosophy:
A. The Pre-WWII/Post WWII time frame
B. The time frame when WWII "baby boomers" started to think about retirement

You can see by the bar graph that institutional pension plans, in some form, have been with us since our nation's beginning. In the private sector they were established as employer/employee promises most often with no formal annuity structure. Pensions were simply a promise that if you worked until a certain age, you could be given some type of pension allowance. Things started to change, taking on governmental involvement in 1926, with passage of the Railway Labor Act. In the early 1900s railroads were the key industry in the U.S. and dependence on railroads for transportation and freight was of national importance. Also, at this time, there were hundreds of independent railroad companies operating in the U.S., competing for services. Not all railroad companies operated with adequate respect for the human component of the industry. Adequate safety standards were not in place, and train accidents were frequent and deadly. Compensation and working conditions (among other matters) for railroad workers were inconsistent between railroad companies, and many of those programs were established in such an arbitrary manner that they eventually lead to federal regulatory control. The 1926 Railway Labor Act was designed to cover many employer sins, and with it, the industry pension plan also became law.

In 1935 the National Labor Relations Act (NLRA) was passed that established labor standards (minimum wage, hours of work, overtime . . .) and legally introduced the collective bargaining process to the private sector. The resulting, third party, collective bargaining process established many new private pension plans. It is apparent to me that in 1935 our legislature recognized it would not be possible to have separate labor laws for every industry (e.g. Railroad Industry Labor Law, Trucking Industry Labor Law, Electrical Industry Labor Law . . .) and the NLRA was designed as an answer.

The Social Security Act was also passed in 1935 extending government-regulated pension coverage to workers throughout the U.S. Here the plan philosophy and financial support was based on contributions made by both the company and employee with the federal government in control, managing the plan. One out-growth of this dual contribution arrangement was that many private pension plans began to link (integrate) their plan benefits to the benefits allowed under social security.

Later, in 1947, with the passage of the Taft-Hartly Act, pension and benefit plans for multi-employer groups (e.g. construction, trucking) were given legal foundation.

Many private sector plans continued to offer retirement benefits to individuals and groups of employees as part of their benefit program. These very often were merely pension promises that lacked funding or annuity structure. Many of the pension plans became too much to manage in the private sector, resulting in a transfer of the administrative responsibility to insurance companies in the form of annuity contracts. Open-ended annuities were established to allow new entries to this annuity configuration as people in the organization reached retirement and would be then added to the insurance annuity contract retirement plan. Generally each year the insurance provider would need to renegotiate annuity contracts that were not for a fixed group of retired workers. To be able to add new retirees to an existing annuity the insurance pension provider needed additional capital to cover the benefits paid, administrative costs, and some extra capital for profit. Somewhere along the way, companies started to take back the pension plans to save money by administering the plans in-house. No need to pay the high annuity expenses and insurance profit margins when the work could be done cheaper in-house.

This arrangement worked fine until some companies found it financially impossible to maintain their pension plans, and then simply dropped the benefit offering. This left many workers suddenly out in the cold without a pension. Workers who had relied on their company pension promise were abandoned and left holding the proverbial empty bag.

Early in my career I met many of these unfortunate people. Sadly, some had worked thirty or more years with a company, and when their manufacturing plant closed, they were told that the pension plan was a plant location plan. Since the plant closed, there would be no pension. It was tough, heart-breaking news for anyone and in the late 1960s and early 1970s but it was not an uncommon occurrence.

A very big pension-close debacle occurred when the Studebaker Automobile Company closed its doors. Studebaker had been a long-standing U.S. corporation that actually started out making Conestoga covered wagons used by pioneers traveling into the, then unexplored, western USA. As time past the company evolved into a major automobile manufacturer. When Studebaker shut down their company pension plan, the shut down affected thousands of workers and existing retirees. Retirees receiving monthly pensions were told that the payments would end, and those workers at Studebaker who held the company pension promise were told the promise was basically worthless. Try as they did, Studebaker workers never recovered their pension promise.

Bad management got attention, and false pension promises (not just Studebaker) lead to the passage of the Employee Retirement Income Security Act (ERISA) of 1974 (effective 1976). ERISA was designed as a cure to private pension shortfalls; it established eligibility, vesting, and funding standards that would be regulated by the Department of Labor (DOL) and the Internal Revenue Service (IRS). ERISA also formed the Pension Benefit Guarantee Corporation (PBGC), a semi-government company that would oversee and "guarantee" private pension plans and work to ensure their growth.

Important to note that while ERISA was desperately needed to repair the integrity of private pension plans and (by law) foster the growth of new plans, the opposite is now taking place. After many years of governmental involvement, defined benefit pension plans have evolved into programs that are prodigious, complex, and costly. The regulators (DOL, IRS, PBGC and our legislature) mandate plan standards that require legal and actuarial expenses that can, at times, be unbearable. Instead of fostering growth, ERISA now orchestrates substantial pension decline. The benefit "guarantee" provided by the PBGC is starting to look more like a Studebaker pension promise, as the PBGC systematically cuts pension benefits that have been promised to private sector workers.

Private sector defined benefit plans, unfortunately, are a vanishing breed of pensions, disappearing at a rapid and accelerating rate from the corporate scene. The 2006 Pension Protection Act (PPA) was designed to help reverse that downward trend by, among other things, establishing new funding standards and new plan restrictions. It is this writer's sincere wish that PPA reaches that end and will foster private pension growth, but I fear that PPA represents action taken, too little too late. Defined Benefit (DB) Pension Plans - RIP.

While I have a heartfelt (and personal) appreciation for private pension plans, if I were to start my own company, I would not offer a defined benefit pension plan to my employees. The cost to set up and operate a defined benefit plan far exceeds any benefits my company or employees would receive. Those plan expenses represent costs that never go away, and benefit plan money that is available can be put to better use. Most importantly, it is not likely that I would be able to find customer dollars to pay for a defined benefit pension plan. Remember: All dollars are customer dollars.

Key points and final comments on this subject:
- If you do not have a qualified defined benefit program, don't start one and if you have one in place, start looking for a way out ("real" hunting).

- Aggressively employ outside professional services (administration, trust management, investment management and actuarial support) and measure (SPC) their performance [guide].

401K PLANS

401k plans (called defined contribution plans) are, presently, much less expensive, easier to manage, and less complex to administer. Here too the benefits derived from them for both the company and their employees can be great. It becomes a retirement benefit partnership between the employee and employer with benefit portability in the event of job change or job loss. 401k plans will soon become the primary private employer pension program.

It is my opinion that most of the work needed to support and to manage 401k plans should be contracted out and done by a specialized outside service company. Doing the investment and administrative work in-house (correctly and efficiently) can easily exceed the talent of any HR staff. As example, years ago, I managed my company 401k plan in-house, but doing it in-house represented an out-of-balance financial drain on company assets. The process got mired down in a constant quagmire of administrative problems. The plan design was very good, but the administrative grief was endless. Consequently, my company was not happy with the plan (costs high and results low), employees were not happy with the plan (perception), and most of all I was very unhappy with the plan and its seemingly endless administrative grief. Tremendous amounts of time, talent, and money went into designing a very good 401k plan, but the plan was not recognized as strong because of the many administrative complexities.

I took time to study and evaluate several outside providers and selected the Vanguard Group to bundle up and manage the entire 401k plan for our company. This was absolutely the best HR decision I ever made in my entire career. The Vanguard organization did a superior job from the very beginning and overnight the administrative grief disappeared. People throughout the company suddenly saw our 401k plan as an excellent retirement savings program and a great company benefit. Keep in mind that the plan design did not change, only plan administration changed. It was managed outside by people who were very skilled professionals in that specific business. Let me add that this transfer of administrative grief to Vanguard also trimmed our 401k operating and administrative costs (banking fees, trust service fees, advisory fees) by nearly sixty percent. Hey, not too bad! Vanguard was a class act of a company with an established culture in place that was truly focused on their customers. If any HR mangers out there want some positive ideas on how to manage people in a large organization, just take time to watch the Vanguard Team, they were outstanding then and I think that performance culture continues.

Key points and final comments on this subject:
- Recognize the tremendous value of a 401k benefit plan and design a program that matches your needs (hunt).
- Employ outside professional services (do not entertain in-house administration) and measure their performance (SPC) [guide].

DESIGN PHILOSOHY

As you design your employee benefit package every component of the plan must marry well with an overall design philosophy (each organization establishes it's own). There is one design philosophy that I must recommend for consideration. It is the philosophy of front-end loading. Use your benefit package to attract and retain talent by offering benefit qualifications at the beginning of the employment scenario. If you offer three weeks of vacation upon the completion of five years of service, consider moving that up to the first year with a week of vacation available after six months service (borrowed from the three). If you have 401k vesting (for a company match) after three years or a progressive match over several years, look to move vesting forward into year one. Examine all benefit offerings that have a delayed vesting or eligibility and consider moving the vesting/delay forward.

A business cost analysis is needed but remember to factor in the cost of turnover. This new synergized world carries with it turnover expenses that may be gigantic.

Front-end loading of a benefit program will help retain the talent your organization has (hopefully) worked hard to secure. Individuals well matched on the job will be less inclined to depart voluntarily if they know all benefit plans would then start over. Think about it – just and idea.

Briefly stated, HR needs to provide a comprehensive employee benefit package that will help attract and retain talent (that is the most important HR role) by designing and delivering benefit plan products that are competitive (not the highest) and cost competitive. Employees must also perceive the benefit package offered by the company as being fair.

CHAPTER 16

EMPLOYEE BETTERMENT

In HR the key responsibility is to recruit and retain the talent needed to make products or services for the customer. Once in place those new employees need to be given direction and assistance for continued growth and betterment (personal and professional). Recruiting is goal number 1 and betterment is goal number 2.

For health care betterment here are two very positive programs that organizations need to consider. These programs can also be designed and administrated at a very low cost:

1. Set up some form of a physical exercise program or exercise area and complement that program with some type of annual physical evaluation. There are dozens of ways to do this, they can be done at low cost, and this scenario sends a message to your workers that they need to take care of themselves and that you do care about their physical

conditioning (maybe yes and maybe no). It is hard to measure, but I am confident that health management programs go far to reduce health care costs.

2. You will need an Employee Assistance Program (EAP) if you have one hundred employees or more. With one hundred or more employees you will have some type of non-work human problem (personal, financial or family problem) that will adversely affect your workers, their productivity, and the complexity of the problems may exceed your imagination. The EAP needs to be managed outside your company, in a confidential setting and run by counseling professionals. Do not try to manage non-work people problems in-house, it is not your business, it can be very expensive, and truthfully few if any HR/management people are qualified to work in this area.

As an example of a need for EAP's I'll share a true story. At my last employer we had EAP's at all locations absent one large twelve hundred employee location. The general manager of this location was a good person and very good manager but would not consider setting up an EAP. He had personally gone through some very difficult times and was a single parent with two daughters in high school. His position was that if he was able to manage all the hard times that came his way then anyone else could do it just as easily. That was not at all true however the HR director and I were unsuccessful on several tries to convince the general manager otherwise. Well, with twelve hundred employees in the organization, non-work problems were present, and unfortunately, in a very short time period two separate and serious non-work problems lead to employee suicides. Soon after the second suicide the HR director and I were given the green light to set up an EAP program. I firmly believe that if you have one hundred or more employees, you need some form of EAP. Do not do EAP work in-house.

TRAINING AND DEVELOPMENT

Without question my favorite part of the HR management business is training and development (T&D). It is the primary area where leaders provide the organization and the people in the organization an opportunity to learn and grow. The training discipline is viewed as important by employees as (if nothing else) a sign that the company cares. If the company cares about employee growth, the employees will respond in kind. Betterment goes both ways. It is easy logic that if employees believe that the company cares, they too will care, and that can only result in better job performance. Every organization needs to learn, grow, and change direction with new ideas, new insight, and imagination if it is to survive. Employees also know, in this synergizing business world, that they need to continue to develop their skills to preserve jobs and careers going forward. A well established training program that is supported by top management is the tool to help make this happen.

Here I want to share with you three training programs I used that were given A+ ratings and were programs that directly supported our business and our customers. I will also share an idea I had for a forth training program that by circumstance (as Curly Howard would say) never came to fruition.

Program Number 1: I had Herb Cohen teach managers a negotiations class on three separate occasions to help managers learn more about the process of negotiations - an important component of every manager's job. Those training seminars could only be described as excellent and were always completed with 100 percent success. Herb's two books are ones I consider must-reading for any manager. His first and a number one best seller was titled You Can Negotiate Anything, his second, Negotiate This. Herb's negotiation presentations were very captivating, they were fun, and magnificent learning experiences. The Herb Cohen seminars provided direct benefits to our company, our customers, and each seminar participant. Any person who participated in one of the Herb Cohen Seminars will tell you that they remember well Herb's rewarding training presentation. I am personally and professionally in debt to Herb Cohen as he served as one of my best business guides. Thanks to Herb, I gradually learned, among other things, to: "Care, but not too much!"

Program Number 2: I have had the tremendous pleasure of working with Dr. David L. Cooperrider, PhD of Case Western Reserve University in Cleveland, Ohio. Dr. Cooperrider's training program (and book) is titled Appreciative Inquiry. He does an unbelievable job of getting groups of any size to work together very positively and constructively. Dr. Cooperrider is a phenomenal person who presented training programs at my company that were inspiring and valuable beyond description, and he is one of the most positive individuals I have ever met. At one meeting Dave shared with me a study on positive feedback that I must pass along.

In this example a study was undertaken that involved training two groups of people on how to bowl at a bowling alley. All the participants in this study were people who had never gone bowling or had minimal knowledge of the game. The participants were separated into two large groups that were equal demographically (size, sex, age, etc.) and were given equal training instruction and time that included video performance reviews. One group however only received positive feedback (strikes and spares) from the instructors advising them what they were doing right, ignoring their mistakes. The second group only received negative feedback (gutter balls and poor form) advising them of what they were doing wrong, ignoring those things they did right. At the end of the training these two groups entered into bowling competition and as you might imagine the positive feedback group won each contest. They not only won the games, they won by large margins and were superior in every single category that could be used to measure the sport of bowling. The two groups were not even close.

Think about this study and how you might respond if, for example, you have a child come home with a report card and all the grades received are very good absent one. If you are like me (and most others) your eyes and actions will only focus on the one bad grade. What was wrong and not what was right. It's best to place focus on the things done right.

Dr. Cooperrider is also an excellent guide with a fantastic ability to frame his guidance very positively with lasting results.

<u>Program Number 3</u>: This one might sound a little bizarre, but trust me, it was a valuable and great training experience. I hired a poet named David Whyte to speak to management groups on two separate occasions. David wrote a book titled <u>The Heart Aroused</u> and is referred to by many major U.S. companies as the corporate poet. David had memorized over one hundred poems, and he recited many of them in a unique and skillful way that energized the groups and stimulated creative thought. He was a great person to listen to and did a fantastic job of getting managers to think outside the box. I highly recommend David and his enlightened training approach even though, as a poet, he is not too impressed that my favorite poet happens to be Robert W. Service.

David Whyte serves as a guide as well and a very good one too, using poetry as the medium to open minds and kindle thought.

<u>Program Number 4</u>: Now this one was a training activity that I planned but was never able to implement. Here I wanted to introduce art as a medium to kindle inventive ideas and inspire imagination

at the top of our organization. Using art, primarily sketching and watercolor, I wanted to have a local high school or college art teacher train key executives in the basics of art and then see what they would or could imagine and create. One project would have been a contest for executives to paint a picture of our customers. That's right, just paint a picture of our customers . . . abstract, modern, or whatever. Hey, it's the litany from the top that sells ideas and generates energy at the bottom and throughout an organization. What better, more creative way can there be than to express it in art form? So many of those uninspiring mission statements hanging on the corporate wall are never read or believed by workers at any level of the organization, but employees in the organization might take time to look at and think about this artwork and the meaning behind it. Imagine, the top executive "paints" a picture of the customer! Somebody out there try it, and let me know how it turns out.

Let me re-emphasize that it is critical to get management support and involvement from the very top of the organization. Without involvement from the most influential leaders in your organization, you can only struggle with development programs that too often only achieve mediocre results. Somehow HR needs to develop top management talent to become leadership guides for the business. Leaders can be, and often are, great hunters. They must also serve as guides for the organization to succeed.

Key points and final comments on this subject:

- Recognize that employee betterment programs represent the future of the organization. Without employee betterment, there is no future (organizations must have guides).
- Measure results of employee betterment activities (SPC).

Well, folks, here you have it. Everything you ever wanted to know about HR management capsulated into two chapters of this book. Yes, over thirty-five years of HR management experience here for the reading.

Please do not misinterpret any of the casual remarks I've made about HR in this book as demeaning toward the discipline. HR management should not to be ridiculed as it is a serious and complex discipline that only gets more complex as we move forward with our fully synergized organizations.

I have seen monumental changes in the HR discipline over the years - complex changes that consistently place greater demands on HR practitioners. I also recognize it as a critical business discipline, arguably the most critical because without motivated human assets in an organization, that organization will be useless. I saw a drawing once in a magazine that I thought clearly dramatized the need for motivated human assets. In this drawing there was a football team on the field, lined up, and prepared for the opening game kick-off. On the opposing side there were no players, only empty team jerseys and empty shoes in place where the players should be. Without motivated people in place, learning and growing, nothing gets done. It is the primary responsibility of the HR department to recruit, motivate, and retain the talent needed to provide products and/or services that meet customer requirements. Empty jerseys and empty shoes cannot supply the customer with goods and services.

REFLECTIONS ON LEADERSHIP AND PEOPLE MANAGEMENT

Leadership is much more than simply a title bestowed on an individual. Leadership carries with it authority, and with that authority leaders are called on to make decisions. Not all decisions are easy to make, nor are all decisions viewed with favor by those affected once a decision is made.

In the working world true leaders must train and position themselves to make decisions and lead.

Let me take a moment to reflect back on comments made by behavioral scientist Douglas McGregor regarding leadership authority and the need for leaders to make decisions. McGregor served for a few years as president of Antioch College in Ohio, and at the time of his departure from Antioch he made these interesting observations in his final note to the alumni and faculty.

> " I believed, for example, that a leader could operate successfully as a kind of advisor to his organization. I thought I could avoid being a 'boss.' Unconsciously, I suspect, I hoped to duck the unpleasant necessity of making difficult decisions, of taking the responsibility for one course of action, among many uncertain alternatives, of making mistakes and taking the consequences. I thought that maybe I could operate so that everyone would like me, that 'good human relations' would eliminate all discord and disagreement.
>
> I couldn't have been more wrong. It took a couple of years, but I finally began to realize that a leader cannot avoid the exercise of authority any more than he can avoid responsibility for what happens to his organization."

You see leaders first and foremost need to make good decisions, and not all leaders are fully prepared when decision time arrives. Leaders can vacillate, procrastinate, shove responsibility onto others, whatever, but in the end a decision must be made and those leaders who can be decisive are the certified leaders of the organization. It is interesting too that very often the certified leaders do not sit at the top of an organization. I suspect that sometimes us folks at the top are too busy putting up "don't lean signs."

When employees have questions on organizational direction they go to the individuals who they recognize as the leaders, and I submit that those are the leaders who are very skilled hunters and guides. Look around your organization and try to determine who is sought out by employees when key questions surface on the direction your organization is taking. Your search might render a few surprises.

In any leadership position it is important to acknowledge the need to continually hone your natural hunting skills by embracing the concept of lifetime learning, as Henry Ford said: "to keep your mind young." First, leaders must recognize that nothing is stagnant in business, and in every area of business (including people) there is an ongoing and ever changing requirement to collect more information, ask more questions, listen more attentively to what is being said and plan a course of action (make decisions). Second, leaders at every level of an organization need to teach themselves how to recognize those opportunities where they can reach out and serve as guides enabling others to achieve unimagined results.

In business it is positive leadership (hunting, guiding and decisiveness) that makes organizations stronger, more productive, and able to keep those customers happy. Continue to remind yourself that in the end it is the customer who pays all the bills - the customer, the customer, the customer.

I hope you enjoyed reading my book finding my reflections on business hunting and guiding helpful for your business career. Good luck to you in future hunting and guiding endeavors.

Keep the wind in your favor,
Bill Wonders

References and works cited

Alaska Atlas and Gazetteer, Anchorage, Alaska, DeLorme Mapping, 1992.

Alaska Geographic, Anchorage, Alaska, Voume 25, Number 4, 1998.

David Attenborough, *Life on Earth*, Little, Brown & Co., Boston, Mass, 1980.

Tom Brokaw, *The greatest generation*, Random House, NY, 2005

Herb Cohen, *You can negotiate anything*, Bantam Books, Secaucus, NY, 1988 and *Negotiate This*, Warner Books, New York, 2003.

Stan Cohen, *The trail of '42*, Pictorial Histories Publishing Co, Inc., Missoula, Montana, 2006.

Dermot Cole, *Frank Barr Bush Pilot in Alaska and the Yukon*, Alaska Northwest Publishing Co., Edmunds, Washington, 1986.

David L. Cooperrider, Peter F. Sorensen, Jr., Diana Whitnew, Therese F. Yaeger, *Appreciative inquiry*, Stipes Publishing, Champaign, Ill. 2000.

Rich Hackenberg, *Moose hunting in Alaska*, Northern Press, Wasilla, AK, 2004.

Sparky Imeson, *Mountain Flying*, Airguide Publications, Long Beach, CA, 1987.

Eugene E. Jennings, *An Anatomy of Leadership,* McGraw-Hill Book Company, NY NY, 1972.

James Kavanagh and Raymond Leung, *The night sky*, Waterford Press, Phoenix, AZ, 2001.

Steven Levi and Jim O'Meara, *Bush flying*, TAB Books, Blue Ridge Summit, PA,1992.

Abraham H. Maslow, *Eupsychian Management,* Richard D. Irwin Inc. and The Dorsey Press, Homewood, Ill, 1965.

Douglas McGregor, *The Human Side of Enterprise,* McGraw-Hill Book Co.,Inc. NY NY, 1960, *Leadership and Motivation*, The MIT Press, Cambridge, MA, 1966, *The Professional Manager,* McGraw-Hill Book Co., NY NY, 1967.

Ron Miller and William K. Hartman, *The grand tour guide to the solar system*, Workman Publishing, New York, 2005.

M. Scott Myers, *Every Employee a Manager,* McGraw-Hill Book Company, NY NY, 1970.

F.E. Potts, *Guide to bush flying,* ACS Publishing, Tucson, AZ, 1993.

Robert W. Service, *The best of Robert Service*, Perigee Books, New York, 1953, *The very best of Robert Service*, Todd Communications, Anchorage, AK, 2002 and poems provided that have been posted on-line.

Bill Skinner, Jr., *Moose – Giant of the northern forest,* Firefly Books, Buffalo, NY 1998.

Dr. Dave Smith, Quote provided in a personal meeting at the Southern Park Tavern, Youngstown, Ohio in 1971.

Aleksandr Solzhenitsyn, *One day in the life of Ivan Denisovich.* Farrar, Staus and Giroux, New York, 1991.

Ross Stagner, *The Gullibility of Personnel Managers*, Personnel Psychology, Inc., 1958.

Lawrence L. Steinmetz, *Nice Guys Finish Last,* Horizon Publications, Inc. Boulder, CO, Devin-Adair Publishers, Old Greenwich, CT, 1983.

Irving Stone, *Dear Theo*, Signet Books, New York, 1969

Edward J. Tarbuck and Frederick K. Lutgens, *Earth Science*, Prentice Hall, Upper Saddle River, NJ, 1997.

US Army Survival Manual FM - 21, Barnes and Noble/Platinum Press, USA, 1992.

Will Tirion, *Smithsonian/Collins Star finder guide and planisphere*, Harper Collins Publishing, New York, 2006.

Lilly Tomlin, Henry Ford, Benjamin Franklin, Yogi Berra, Will Rogers, Dr. Martin Luther King, General George S. Patton, Casey Stengel, Will Rogers, Curly Howard - Quotes taken from business bulletins, newsletters, flyers, newspapers and magazines over the years and specific source not authoritatively documented.

David Whyte, *The heart aroused*, Doubleday Publishing, New York, 1996.

About the Author

Bill Wonders holds an MBA degree with over thirty-five years experience in human resource management and general business management. He recently retired from Gould Electronics Inc. as vice president of human resources and currently serves as president of Woods and Water LLC. Bill has written a wide array of internal and external business publications as well as aviation articles and articles on outdoor recreation.

Orion Too is his first book and a manuscript for a second book Hunter or Hunted, North 63.50 West 147.50, is currently under way.